A Blessed Lent

Meditations on the Readings and Prayers of the Mass

by
Fr Philip G. Bochanski, C.O.

*All booklets are published thanks to the
generous support of the members of the
Catholic Truth Society*

CATHOLIC TRUTH SOCIETY
PUBLISHERS TO THE HOLY SEE

Contents

All rights reserved. First published 2014 by The Incorporated Catholic Truth Society, 40-46 Harleyford Road London SE11 5AY. Tel: 020 7640 0042 Fax: 020 7640 0046. © 2014 The Incorporated Catholic Truth Society.

Inside images: *Seven Virtues attributed to workshop of Pesellino* © Corbis.

ISBN 978 1 86082 899 7

Introduction

One of the lasting fruits of the Great Jubilee is the third edition of the *Roman Missal*, which was published in Latin in 2000 and has now been translated for English-speaking Catholics around the world. In addition to some modifications to the texts and rubrics for the celebration of Holy Mass, the *Missal* also enriches the Church's liturgy with new Mass prayers to celebrate the feasts of the saints and to call on divine assistance in various circumstances.

The third edition of the *Roman Missal* contains a particular gift to the Church for the season of Lent, the six weeks between Ash Wednesday and Holy Thursday that are set aside for penance in preparation for Easter. Following an ancient liturgical tradition, the *Missal* provides a solemn prayer of blessing, called the *Prayer over the People*, for every day in Lent.

Similar prayers for the end of Holy Mass are found in the earliest centuries of the Church, in the ancient liturgies of Christians in Syria and Egypt as well as in Rome. In fact, many of the *Prayers over the People* that appear in the present *Missal* are drawn directly from our oldest Latin liturgical texts, including the *Sacramentary* of Pope Gelasius (AD 492-96). Other ancient manuscripts attest to the importance of these solemn blessings, especially in Masses celebrated by the Holy Father. Pope Gregory the Great (AD 535-604) decreed that they would be used at each Mass from Ash Wednesday to Wednesday of Holy Week, a practice that continued in force until the revision of the *Missal* in 1969. The restoration of these prayers to the *Missal* - mandatory for the Sundays of Lent, and optional for weekdays - provides an opportunity to reflect on the nature of Lent, and on the way the Church responds to it.

These forty days are meant to be a time of reflection and of special preparation for the renewal of baptismal promises that will take place at Mass at Easter. Just as those preparing for Baptism as adults undergo a period of purification before they receive the Sacraments, all of the faithful are annually invited to continuing conversion in light of the coming "anniversary" of their rebirth in Christ. During Lent, each Christian is called to examine his moral life, especially the manner in which he observes the two Great Commandments of love for God and love for neighbour. Together the faithful join in the penitential practices enjoined on them by the Lord himself: prayer, fasting and almsgiving.

Thus, Lent becomes a time of spiritual combat, as each of us strives to overcome the temptations of the Devil and the drives of the body, and to live more fully for God. This is not an easy task, so the Church reaches out to her children, in the midst of their spiritual exertions and physical fatigue, with support and encouragement. After feeding them with the Bread of Life, the Eucharist, the Church sends her children back into the world with prayers that beg God to protect them from evil and strengthen them for doing good.

There is no shortage of books to assist the Catholic faithful with meditations and reflections for the season of Lent. Like many others, this little text draws on the passages from Scripture assigned for each day's liturgy, which are replete with the words of the prophets and the teaching of the Lord Jesus. But our reflections will also make use of the precious gift of the *Prayers over the People*, whose petitions will provide the lens through which we interpret the daily Word of God. By considering both the prayers and the readings with faith and devotion, we will be able to enter more fully into the liturgies of these days of preparation, in company with the faithful around the world and throughout history. As we hear the Church, our Mother, pray to God the Father on our behalf, we can enter more deeply into communion with them both.

Note on the Text

The *Prayer over the People* for each day's Mass is provided at the beginning of each meditation. Words in the meditation that are taken from or based on the *Prayer over the People* are printed in italics.

Ash Wednesday

Pour out a spirit of compunction, O God,
on those who bow before your majesty,
and by your mercy may they merit the rewards
    you promise
to those who do penance.
Through Christ our Lord.

Jl 2:12-18; Ps 51; 2 Co 5:20-6:2; Mt 6:1-6,16-18

⚭

Compunction is not a word that we use often in everyday life. It comes from the Latin word *pungere*, which means "to poke"; it is from this root that we derive words like *puncture* and *point*. *Compungere* means to poke hard, to poke sharply. Thus, compunction is the "poke" that the conscience gives to the will - to spur a person on to do good, to warn him of impending evil, or to remind him of past faults. It is the way that the conscience points him in the right direction. This makes compunction a good watchword for Lent, the season when we strive to overcome past sins and find a clear path to the Lord.

Today's Gospel reveals another kind of poking, which can lead to *rewards* for *those who do penance*. In the Sermon on the Mount, the Lord Jesus explains that penance is good and salutary, if it is carried out in a certain way. It is from this text that we derive the three classic penitential practices of Lent: fasting, almsgiving and prayer. The three are intimately connected: it is impossible to fast or give alms unless we are committed to prayer.

Fasting pokes at a person because it involves the needs and desires of the body. When your empty stomach growls and pokes at you for attention, it is a reminder to pray for perseverance and the renewal of the relationship between the body and the soul. When abstinence pokes at the memory - "What day is it? Can I eat that today?" - it is a call to pray for humility and a generous spirit, which makes us willing to *bow before the majesty of God*, and to submit to the teaching of the Church. Fasting and abstinence are not simply personal good works, but must be done in a spirit of solidarity with all our fellow believers.

Almsgiving also pokes at the heart. When the plight of a brother or sister in need of our material or spiritual assistance pokes at our attention, it is a beneficial moment to pray for a deeper charity. When our wallet or purse is empty because we have been generous, it is time to pray in thanksgiving for the good things we have, and for the opportunity to share them.

The penance that we carry out during Lent is not an end in itself: its *rewards* are found in its fruits. Penance does not merely poke at the soul, but also points the way. Fasting and almsgiving must always lead to prayer, and prayer points the way to a deeper relationship with God. This relationship was formed in us at Baptism, when we made the promises that we will renew forty days hence in our celebration of Easter. The *spirit of compunction* prods us along the path which leads to that joyous moment, and points out the obstacles along that path, which our Lenten penance can remove.

Thursday after Ash Wednesday

Almighty God,
who have made known to your people
the ways of eternal life,
lead them by that path, we pray,
to you, the unfading light.
Through Christ our Lord.

Dt 30:15-20; *Ps* 1; *Lk* 9:22-25

Today's *Prayer over the People* brings to mind an image from the story of the Exodus - the pillar of fiery cloud by which God led the Israelites for forty years, day and night, through the Sinai desert to the Land of Promise. It marked out the way for them, and told them when to move and where to stop. Its *unfading light* allowed them to journey even at night, and reassured the people of the Lord's presence in their midst and of his protection.

The First Reading today is from the conclusion of Moses' farewell address to the children of Israel, now that they have reached their destination. Moses is not going to cross the Jordan River with them into the Promised Land, but he warns the people to stay on the *path* that the Lord marked out for them: the way of blessing, the way of life.

Moses tells them how to have a long life; in fact he *makes known to* God's *people the ways of eternal life*: "Love the Lord your God, obeying his voice, clinging to him."

The way of life, then, is marked by a deep love of God, submission to his will, and persevering trust in his plan. This is another way to say *love, faith and hope*, the theological virtues that are infused along with sanctifying grace. They are given first at Baptism, and renewed in the other Sacraments. We must exercise them every day if we are to walk the path of discipleship.

The Gospel reading finds Jesus on his own path, which will be the way of eternal life for his disciples and for all of us. But he tells those who follow him that it will be a way marked by rejection, suffering and death. More than that, he warns his disciples - then and now - that they must not just watch him walk this way, but take up their own crosses, accept their own suffering, and walk this path in his footsteps.

Jesus gave his disciples plenty of notice, describing exactly what would lie ahead, and precisely what would be required of them. They had plenty of time to decide whether they would follow him or not. This Lent, the question is put to us as well: can we, will we, walk this way with him?

It can only be done if we follow the same path that Moses pointed out. We can only follow him if we have a deep conviction of God's love for us, and a willingness to respond to him in love. We need faith that knows and believes that the loving God knows what he is about, and that willingly follows and submits to the plans of divine Providence. We must have that firm hope in God's love, in his plan and in his help that enables us to persevere in following him all the way along the path that leads to the cross.

Jesus tells us that the Way of the Cross leads to Resurrection, and it is in his Easter glory that he is revealed as our *unfading light* along the *ways of eternal life*. Through the seriousness and penance of Lent we arrive at the festival of Easter. On the often dark path of daily suffering, we reach the brightness of eternal light.

Friday after Ash Wednesday

For your mighty deeds, O God of mercy,
may your people offer endless thanks,
and by observing the age-old disciplines
along their pilgrim journey,
may they merit to come and behold you forever.
Through Christ our Lord.

Is 58:1-9a; *Ps* 51; *Mt* 9:14-15

∞

We come today to the first "meatless" Friday of Lent, the first day of communal abstinence. Hopefully our individual Lenten sacrifices, our personal "giving up", has also lasted at least this long! It is a wonderful thing that the Church retains the tradition of giving things up (fasting) and taking things on (almsgiving and prayer) during this season of Lent. But for these practices to be beneficial to us, we have to look at them from the proper perspective.

The *Prayer over the People* at the end of today's Mass reminds us that it is God who carries out the *mighty deeds* in our lives and our relationship with him. We have a more simple way marked out for us: simply to keep *the age-old disciplines* and to walk the *pilgrim journey* that has been well trodden for generations. We follow this path of penance in solidarity with countless generations before us, and with millions of our fellow Catholics around the world.

Our common penance, our shared rules for fasting and almsgiving, not only help us personally as individuals, but also keep us united to the community of faith that is the Church. Isaiah reminds us, though, that as good as these external penances are, they are not enough. Rather, he insists that outward works must always lead to inner change, and while we may shrink a bit in the body as a result of fasting, the heart and soul ought to grow larger and larger, full of love towards the helpless and generosity for the needy.

In this way we may *come and behold* Christ, as we recognise him present in every person who asks for help, and we serve him in loving them. Even though Jesus is not visible to the bodily eye, and seems, in the words of the Gospel, to have been "taken away", through this kind of fasting - this kind of loving - we behold him in our brothers and sisters, and we can rejoice with him, even as we fast.

Saturday after Ash Wednesday

Abide graciously, O Lord, with your people,
who have touched the sacred mysteries,
that no dangers may bring affliction
to those who trust in you, their protector.
Through Christ our Lord.

Is 58:9b-14; *Ps* 86; *Lk* 5:27-32

∽

Yesterday, we were considering the Lenten practice of fasting. Today's readings speak of eating: specifically, about people sharing food with one another.

Isaiah speaks in the name of the Lord (we are resuming right where yesterday's reading left off) and says that one of the things that the Lord expects is that his people "bestow [their] bread on the hungry". He doesn't say, "find bread for the hungry", or "make some bread", or even "share some of your bread", but simply, "give your bread". That is, he expects us to give away what we have, the very thing on which we are relying for our own strength and security.

Perhaps we are talking about fasting after all! But Isaiah insists that to bestow one's bread comes with a reward: he goes on to say that the Lord, who *abides graciously with his people* "will guide you, giving you relief … will give strength to your bones … [and] will feed you". So, there is a reward in store for those who are generous. Still, how does one find the courage to give away the very thing that seems necessary for one's own life?

Consider Levi in the Gospel reading: although he left much of what he had at the counting-house, he put on a banquet for the Lord with what he had left. He does this, he makes this sacrifice of his own goods, so that his friends can come to meet Jesus. They are in the same moral situation in which Levi had been, and which he just left at the merciful call of Christ. He has been forgiven, and so he invites his friends to hear the same message of conversion and mercy, and to make the same response.

Here is where we find strength and courage to give ourselves away. Because we have *touched the sacred mysteries* - that is, because we have received the Sacraments - our generosity relies, not merely on the hope of reward, but on the fact that we have already received great gifts. Because, we have been healed in the Sacrament of Reconciliation, we must reach out to others with mercy, and lead people to Jesus. Because we have received the Body and Blood of Christ in the Holy Eucharist, we must give ourselves to others as he has given himself to us, in the bread he bestows on those who hunger for his love.

Then we need never fear *danger* or *affliction* from giving away what little we think we have. The one who abides with us gives us everything we need, and makes it possible for us to be generous in imitation of him.

First Sunday of Lent

May bountiful blessing, O Lord, we pray,
come down upon your people,
that hope may grow in tribulation,
virtue be strengthened in temptation,
and eternal redemption be assured.
Through Christ our Lord.

> Year A: Gn 2:7-9, 3:1-7; Ps 51; Rm 5:12-19; Mt 4:1-11
> Year B: Gn 9:8-15; Ps 25; 1 P 3:18-22; Mk 1:12-15
> Year C: Dt 26:4-10; Ps 91; Rm 10:8-13; Lk 4:1-13

∞

The reading from the Book of Deuteronomy (which is read on this Sunday in Year C), describes the feast of Pentecost, which, before it was connected by Christians with the gift of the Holy Spirit, was a festival to offer the first fruits of field and orchard to the Lord in the Temple. The *Prayer over the People* for this Mass could easily be a part of that ceremony: one reason that the Israelites brought the first part of their harvest to the Lord was to ask that his *bountiful blessing* would *come down* on the rest of their crops, as well as on their houses and families.

In a certain way, this sacrifice of the *first* fruits could not have been easy to make. What the people had in their hands was certain; what was still growing wasn't yet secure. They left home to bring the first fruits to the Lord, and any number of problems could affect their crops while they were away: weeds or diseases; theft or vandalism; locusts and other pests; drought and extreme heat. Even when they were at home, they couldn't *make* the rain fall, or the sun shine, or the winds come from favourable directions. At least at times, it must have been tempting to wait for a while - to make sure that there would be enough for home and family, and take the surplus to be offered to the Lord.

The Devil plays on the same human insecurity in his attempt to seduce Jesus. "Turn these stones into bread," he says. In other words, make your bodily desires the determining factor of whether or not you will serve the Father according to his will. Jesus doesn't waver, but shows us how our efforts to serve the Lord, our habits of *virtue*, may *be strengthened in* time of *temptation*.

Satan tries another tactic. "Bow down to me and I will give you power" - take a shortcut to get what is coming to you anyway. Jesus knows that the way to his kingdom and dominion leads through his Passion and his cross. By accepting this way of humility he shows us how to follow him all the way, knowing that our *eternal redemption* is *assured*.

"Throw yourself down from here" - test God to make sure he will keep *his* promises before you keep yours. But Jesus is absolutely certain of his Father's love and protection, and shows us that this kind of faith in God's love gives us *hope* which *may grow* even in the midst of *tribulation*.

Jesus undergoes his temptations not for himself alone, but to give us an example. As we see him put to the test, we come to know that he understands us, and our thoughts and experiences. By striving to understand him, we can imitate him and his generous, confident, patient service of the Will of God. We can give God the first moments of our day, not hesitating to see what we can spare. We can give him the best of ourselves - our energy, our plans, our talents, our strength - rather than what we have left over after we have taken care of ourselves. We can respond to him immediately, confident in his abundant blessings in the present moment *and* in the future, and give the first fruits of our hearts to him who has given everything to us.

Monday of the First Week of Lent

Enlighten the minds of your people, Lord, we pray,
with the light of your glory,
that they may see what must be done
and have the strength to do what is right.
Through Christ our Lord.

Lv 19:1-2,11-18; *Ps* 19; *Mt* 25:31-46

So far, the readings for Lent have been following a logical progression. Last week, we heard from both Old and New Testaments how to conduct our Lenten penances, especially fasting and almsgiving. The penances we do are supposed to help us to hear the Lord's call to conversion, and to renew our efforts *to do what is right*. Both of today's readings speak of commandments and precepts, so *that* we *may see what must be done*.

These passages are fundamental to our understanding of how to treat our neighbour. In Leviticus 19, Moses relates what has come to be called the "Holiness Code", which includes one of the two Great Commandments: "You shall love your neighbour as yourself." Matthew recounts the Lord's teaching of the corporal works of mercy, which makes this love of neighbour specific, with a list that is repeated four times so that we are sure to learn it. Clearly, then, we can see what must be done. Where will we find the *strength* to do what is right?

These two passages give us, not just rules, but the motivation, the reason, for keeping the rules. "Be holy," the Lord God says, "for I am holy." Be honest, be fair, be patient, be kind, he says, for "I am the Lord" and you belong to me. The Lord *enlightens our minds* so that we can see him in ourselves, so that we can recognise the image of God in which we are created. Because we are made in his image and likeness, we must imitate him and make him visible in our words and actions.

Jesus goes a step further, and challenges us to see *the light of* his *glory* - which is always only visible through the lens of his poverty, his weakness, his suffering - in the faces and lives of our brothers and sisters. We must serve them with compassion - with the same compassion we would hope to show Jesus himself if we met him along the Way of the Cross - because he makes it absolutely clear that he is present in every person, especially the weak and the marginalised.

So, we do what is right because we belong to the Lord, because we recognise his image in ourselves and in others. By serving him in them, we share in the glory of his holiness, as he makes us, more and more visibly, like himself.

Tuesday of the First Week of Lent

May your faithful be strengthened,
O God, by your blessing:
in grief, may you be their consolation,
in tribulation, their power to endure,
and in peril, their protection.
Through Christ our Lord.

Is 55:10-11; *Ps* 34; *Mt* 6:7-15

To grasp the meaning of the First Reading, we need to understand a bit of ancient ecology. When Isaiah relates the Lord's words about the rain and the snow coming down to earth and returning to heaven, he isn't thinking about precipitation and evaporation - the "water cycle" we may have had to learn in school. In his mind, he is imagining the water going down through the earth, to a large basin below and around it - the "waters under the vault" spoken about in the first chapter of the Book of Genesis. From there, it could be let back through openings in the "vault of heaven" to join the "waters above the vault" (as Genesis says) which will fall again as rain.

Isaiah's prophecy tells us that the "water" of God's grace mustn't just fall on his people and keep moving. Rather, like the roots of a plant grasping the rainwater as it seeps through the earth, God's people need to reach out and grasp the grace that God bestows on them, taking it in and making use of it for spiritual growth. In this way they are *strengthened by God's blessing*.

However, since we are persons, not plants, we have a choice to make. Our receiving God's grace must be active and free. So this image points us to a particular pair of petitions in the Lord's Prayer, which Jesus teaches in today's Gospel: "Your kingdom come, your will be done, on earth as in heaven." That God wants to send his "kingdom" - his grace and strength, his will, his presence - into our hearts is clear. We pray the *Our Father* so that we may be aided in our decision to receive and use his grace and strength, in order to bear fruit in our lives.

The fruit that God is looking for from us is challenging. The plants in the Lord's field, watered by his grace, must "give bread for the eating," and bread only comes about when the grain is ground up and transformed by fire. We have to seek and receive God's grace so that we can *endure* the grinding and testing of daily *tribulation*. Then the plant must also provide "seed for the sower," and this requires the death of the plant so that it can give life to new ones. As we die to self each day, God's grace gives us the *consolation* that changes moments of *grief* into gifts of love.

We have to learn this Lent to extend our spiritual roots so we may receive the gift of God's grace, and to plant ourselves deeply and firmly in the love of his kingdom. Then we can do his will and bear good fruit, confident that we have his *protection* in all the *perils* of daily life.

Wednesday of the First Week of Lent

Watch over your people, Lord,
and in your kindness cleanse them from all sins,
for if evil has no dominion over them,
no trial can do them harm.
Through Christ our Lord.

Jon 3:1-10; *Ps* 51; *Lk* 11:29-32

∞

Throughout the Lenten season, we are going to hear the Lord calling us to repentance - in the Gospels, in the writings of the apostles, and especially through his prophets. There are very many calls to conversion in the prophetic books of the Old Testament; more than making predictions, the role of the prophets was to beseech the people to turn again, to turn back to the Law of the Lord and be saved.

Jesus could have quoted any of the famous prophets - Isaiah or Jeremiah, Ezekiel or Hosea - but instead chooses a rather curious prophet called Jonah, who wasn't even sent to the Israelites, but rather to their biggest Gentile enemy. Jesus insists that this message of Jonah is the only "sign" he will give to his listeners. So we have to ask, "Why Jonah?"

Let's take a look at Jonah's mission. In the city of Nineveh, there were so many people, with so many different situations and sins, that Jonah didn't think he would make any impact at all - certainly not for at least the three days it would take to walk the main street of the city from one end to the other. Indeed, if each individual who heard Jonah had simply written him off as a loud, crazy troublemaker, his voice and his message would have gone nowhere.

But two things happened. First, those who heard him along the main road repeated his message to their neighbours and families. It spread like wildfire, and soon the whole populace took it seriously. Then, word got to the king in his palace - the king who was in many ways the leader of the sinfulness of the people - and he couldn't help but take it to heart. The influence of the people and the response of the king led to the conversion of the whole city.

During Lent, we are trying to be open to conversion, asking the Lord to *cleanse us from all sin*, as today's *Prayer over the People* requests. But if we only give attention to this fault or that failing, if we only try to change a few little things that we don't like anyway, we may make small improvements but not real change. What is needed is the willingness to hand over everything to the Lord, especially the hidden sins that we don't like to admit, or the ones that we enjoy too much. In this way, we get to the "king", so to speak - we deal with the *dominion of evil over us*, the attitude of pride or selfishness or anger that is at the root of our sinful actions. When we deal with the king, the rest of the inhabitants of our interior "city" go along, and real change can happen.

This kind of conversion is never easy, to be sure, but the Lord who *watches over his people ... in his kindness* gives us the strength to face the *trials* and sacrifices that lead to salvation and the forgiveness of our sins.

Thursday of the First Week of Lent

May the mercy they have hoped for, O Lord,
come to those who make supplication to you,
and may the riches of heaven be given them,
that they may know what it is right to ask
and receive what they have sought.
Through Christ our Lord.

Est 14:1,3-5,12-14; Ps 138; Mt 7:7-12

It is not difficult to see the common thread between today's two readings, and the psalm as well. They are talking about prayer, and specifically the prayer that is called *supplication* when we seek God's help for ourselves, and *intercession* when we pray on behalf of others. More than that, the readings teach us to pray with confidence, and even with boldness.

Queen Esther in the Old Testament lays out her predicament clearly for the Lord: you must help me, she says to him all day long. "I am about to take my life in my hands," she says. "I am alone and have no helper but you." She remembers how good God has been in the history of her people, and how he always came through for them in moments of crisis. Now in her own difficult situation, she is able to rely on the Lord to help her as well.

Jesus also teaches us to pray confidently, and for the same reason: we know that God is good, and that he loves us, and so we trust him to give us what we need. Certainly we have had the experience, though, of praying for something - really praying hard - and not receiving what we ask for. How can we continue to pray with confidence if God seems not to be listening, or to be letting us down?

Today's *Prayer over the People* gives us some direction: *May the mercy they have hoped for*, it says, *and the riches of heaven, be given* to those *who make supplication* to the Lord - so that, it goes on, *they may know what it is right to ask, and receive what they have sought.* Notice the order of the petitions: we ask God to give us his mercy and the riches of his grace *so that* we will know how to pray, what to ask for. As is always the case with God, his initiative comes first, and we respond.

God always wants to give us the good things that we need: Jesus assures us of this in the Gospel today. If we take the time in meditation and prayer to examine each day and to recognise the blessings that God gives to us, then we may also recognise his plan and his will more clearly. Then we start to pray more and more in harmony with his plan, and we receive what we ask for, what we want, because it is what he wants, too.

Of course we remember that God always hears us, and in his mercy he gives us what we need, which is not always the same as what we want. As we learn to conform more and more to his will, these two things converge, and we pray with confidence and hope of being heard.

Friday of the First Week of Lent

Look with favour on your people, O Lord,
that what their observance outwardly declares
it may inwardly bring about.
Through Christ our Lord.

Ezk 18:21-28; *Ps* 130; *Mt* 5:20-26

"What the Lord does is unjust!" This is the complaint of
the Israelites when they hear of the plans of the Lord for
forgiveness and for judgement. There is a sense, of course,
in which we ought to be very grateful that his way is not
"just". If the Lord dealt with us in terms of strict justice
- if he gave us just what we deserve for our sins - we
would all be in pretty big trouble. Instead, his mercy is
disproportionate to our needs, measured only by his love,
and he forgives us abundantly when we turn back to him.

But this is not what the Israelites meant. They had a
saying, which the Lord rebukes through his prophet: "The
parents have eaten unripe grapes; and the children's teeth
are set on edge" (*Ezk* 18:2; cf. *Jr* 31:29). In other words,
when the Israelites saw illness or misfortune in the life of
an otherwise good person, they said it had to be the result
of a sin of that person's parents. Once a person had sinned

and fallen out of favour with the Lord, then there wasn't any turning back. His destiny was locked in, for himself and his descendants.

This outlook made life easy, in a way. One could figure out a person once and for all - tick the box labelled "sinner" and not worry about him anymore. Life seems easier when everything fits into neat categories. But the Lord rejects this - his ways and his thoughts are different from those of human beings - and he insists that a person's salvation depends, not on someone else's sins or good deeds, but on that person's own cooperation with the Lord and his grace. Thus, every person has a chance to be converted, and we have a responsibility to try to lead each person to the Lord.

Jesus corrects attitudes in a similar way in the Gospel. It is not enough, he says, merely to "observe" the Law of Moses, if *observance* means doing the minimum and being content with *outwardly* satisfying the precepts. What is required for discipleship is a willingness to look deeper - to see mercy underlying justice; to recognise an offender as a brother; to see God's forgiveness in our own lives, and willingly extend forgiveness to others.

This is the fulfilment of the Law, and the beginning of life in Christ - to move from outward observance to *inward* conversion. It means changing, even giving up, our categories, prejudices and plans, and recognising the goodness of a way of life in which mercy triumphs over justice.

Saturday of the First Week of Lent

May the blessing for which they have longed
strengthen your faithful, O God,
so that, never straying from your will,
they may always rejoice in your benefits.
Through Christ our Lord.

Dt 26:16-19; Ps 119; Mt 4:43-48

∞

"*Never straying from* God's *will*"? Really? Never?

As we take stock of the first ten days of Lent, and our progress so far, these words from today's *Prayer over the People* might seem daunting, an admirable but ultimately unattainable goal. Like the first line in today's psalm: "They are happy whose life is blameless." Or, most intimidating, the words of Jesus in today's Gospel: "Be perfect just as your heavenly Father is perfect."

It seems we have two choices here of how to interpret the Scriptures. On the one hand, we can hear the words just quoted as something to keep in mind, maybe something to aspire towards, while deciding that the Lord does not desire to be taken literally. Nobody's perfect, after all - that much seems an axiom of human nature. Surely the Lord wants us to try, even to try really hard, to try our best, but he can't seriously expect perfection, can he?

The other option is to take God at his word - not to shirk the reality that he means what he says, and that what he says is, "Be perfect." If God says it, then it can't be wrong or illogical. More than that: if God says it, then it must be something for our good and for our happiness. He does not set us up to fail.

So how do we reconcile what we have learnt about God's will with what we know about our human condition? Look again at the *Prayer over the People*: *May your blessing ... strengthen your faithful,* it says, *so that, never straying from your will, they may always rejoice.* The blessing comes first - grace allows us and enables us to reach perfection. Likewise, in the First Reading, Moses reminds the people that they have promised to keep all the commandments and ordinances of the Lord. But the Lord has made a promise, too: to be true to his special love for them and to walk with them.

We do not do good things to make God love us. Rather, the fact of God's love for us makes us do good things. Perfection, at its root, means doing the whole thing, walking the whole way. So, we walk with the Lord and find the grace to do good. As we walk with him moment by moment, we have a perfect day. As we walk with him day by day, we make a perfect Lent. As we walk with him month by month, we have a perfect year. We *can* be perfect, as our Father in heaven is perfect, by receiving his love and doing everything in cooperation with him.

Second Sunday of Lent

Bless your faithful, we pray, O Lord,
with a blessing that endures for ever,
and keep them faithful
to the Gospel of your Only Begotten Son,
so that they may always desire and at last attain
that glory whose beauty he showed in his own Body,
to the amazement of his Apostles.
Through Christ our Lord.

Year A: *Gn* 12:1-4a; *Ps* 33; *2 Tm* 1:8b-10; *Mt* 17:1-9
Year B: *Gn* 22:1-2,9a,10-13,15-18; *Ps* 116; *Rm* 8:31b-34; *Mk* 9:2-10
Year C: *Gn* 15:5-12,17-18; *Ps* 27; *Ph* 3:17-4:1; *Lk* 9:28b-36

∞

The story of the Transfiguration is very familiar. It is read on this Sunday of Lent every year, following a long tradition that places the historical event at just about this time before the first Holy Week. The meeting of Jesus with Moses and Elijah amid the cloud of glory has been a subject of sacred art from the days of the earliest icons, through Raphael in the Vatican, down to painters in our own day.

We might ask ourselves, "why those two?" Out of all the possible candidates in the Old Testament - Abraham could surely be one example - why did the Lord choose these

two representatives? One reason is that they encapsulate the Law (Moses) and the Prophets (Elijah), that is, all the places in the Old Testament that foretell the Passion and the Resurrection of Jesus Christ. He will make this point explicit at Easter, when he chides his disciples for being "so slow to believe all that the prophets have said" (*Lk* 24:25). Here, Moses and Elijah signify to the apostles that what is about to happen has long been part of the plan, of the promise of God whose love *endures for ever*.

There is perhaps another reason for the choice of these two, and a particular line in Luke's telling of the story can shed light on it. In that marvellous conversation on Mount Tabor, Luke tells us, "they were speaking of his passing (in Greek, his *exodos*) which he was to accomplish in Jerusalem." "Exodus" in this context makes us think of that historical event, and of another mountain connected with these bright and shining characters: Mount Sinai.

We know very well the story of Moses' encounter with the Lord in the burning bush on Sinai: how God promised to come to the aid of his people and enlisted Moses as his representative. We should recall as well that Moses didn't want the job. He protested that he was a bad speaker, and that the people wouldn't listen to him, and much less would Pharaoh. He insisted that God must have chosen the wrong man. In response, the Lord gave his sacred Name to Moses, so that Moses could call on him, and the Lord promised always to go with Moses and his people.

Elijah also found his way from Israel back to Mount Sinai, pursued by the threats of Queen Jezebel after his confrontation with the prophets of Baal on Mount Carmel. When he arrived there, the Lord asked him, "What are you doing here, Elijah?" (*1 K* 19:9). His response was simple and poignant: he was trying to do the Lord's will, "full of jealous zeal for the Lord of hosts" (*1 K* 19:10), but the way things were working out, he was the only prophet left, and he felt overwhelmed by all that he was up against. Once more, the Lord responded by sending Elijah back to finish his task, having revealed his presence to him and promised his constant support and protection.

In our own lives we are confronted with "Mount Sinai moments", when God's call puts our weaknesses into sharp relief. As we strive to be *faithful to the Gospel*, we can find many excuses that hold us back. Ultimately, though, our vocation is to *always desire and at last attain that glory* that belongs to Jesus by nature, and is offered to us by adoption. By definition this goes beyond our natural abilities, and we have more reasons than Moses or Elijah to protest that we are not up to the challenge. But God's response is the same to us as it was to them: he does not dispute that we are weak - he knows it very well; it's a fact - but rather promises never to leave us, and to give us everything we need to do his will, no matter the obstacles.

For all the *amazement* that the Transfiguration provoked, for all the beautiful works of art it has inspired, the Transfiguration is for doing, not for looking at. The message of Mount Tabor, which we must hear in our Mount Sinai moments, is that the Lord is well aware of our weaknesses and our needs. He has a plan for us, and has committed himself to helping us to fulfil that plan. All is possible for us if we "listen to him".

Monday of the Second Week of Lent

Confirm the hearts of your faithful, O Lord, we pray,
and strengthen them by the power of your grace,
that they may be constant in making supplication to you
and sincere in love for one another.
Through Christ our Lord.

Dn 9:4b-10; *Ps* 79; *Lk* 6:36-38

The prophet Daniel was called to serve the Lord far from his homeland, in the heart of the Babylonian Empire, to which the Israelites had been exiled. In today's First Reading, he assesses the situation of his people, and concludes that their plight is a matter of justice: they have ended up where they are because of their sins. It is a horrible situation, and they don't like it at all, but, Daniel says, "integrity, Lord, is yours," and, in a sense, they deserve the trouble they are in.

An assertion like this can make us uneasy. How could a God who loves us take this kind of approach to dealing with us? How could God, whom we think of as being so merciful, want to exact this kind of justice?

The readings show us, however, that mercy and justice are not contradictory. In fact, a true knowledge of God's merciful love, which *strengthens* us *by the power of* his *grace*, leads us to seek a deeper kind of justice.

Daniel is straightforward about the situation of the Israelites. He is clear about their deeds and what sort of people they have become. But he cries out to the Lord: "To the Lord our God mercy and pardon belong!" He puts the sins of the people in terms not only of transgressions against an external law, but in the light of the covenant relationship. God keeps his covenant, though his people do not; God is faithful, though they have wandered. It is in God's nature to be merciful and to forgive, and in doing so he brings the people back to live as they ought. He restores his image in them.

Jesus takes this a step further. Because the Lord is merciful, he insists, his children must be merciful as well. Because he does not condemn, neither should they. He is forgiving, and so they must forgive others. He is generous, and so they must love from the heart. This is a new kind of justice, based on mercy: we must give to others what we have received from the Lord, and our capacity to receive blessings from him is equal to our capacity to love our neighbour.

Thus, the calculus of God's justice is based on relationships. Our covenant with him and, just as important, our bonds of love and mercy with one another, are the determining factors. This understanding changes the way we pray. As we make *constant supplication* for ourselves, God's answer comes in proportion to our *sincere love for one another*. It must change the way that we live as well, as it is only right and just for us to love as we have been loved.

Tuesday of the Second Week of Lent

Graciously hear the cries of your faithful, O Lord,
and relieve the weariness of their souls,
that, having received your forgiveness,
they may ever rejoice in your blessing.
Through Christ our Lord.

Is 1:10,16-20; *Ps* 50; *Mt* 23:1-12

∞

One cannot get much more blunt about sin than the Lord is
today, speaking through the prophet Isaiah. He is talking to
the Israelites, of course, and their leaders, but he calls them
"rulers of Sodom" and "people of Gomorrah". Using the
names of the most infamous of sinful cities was sure to get
their attention, and shows us just how bad their situation
must have become.

This makes it all the more impressive when we hear
what comes next: "Come now, let us talk this over, says
the Lord." The insistence in his plea, the extent to which
he is willing to go in order to forgive, is extraordinary. It
is as if he said, "Aren't you tired of all this? Isn't it time to
do something about it? What's keeping you from coming
back to me?" We certainly get the sense that, even if the
people didn't quite get it yet, God was certainly weary of
their sinful situation.

Yet, in his weariness, God does not give vent to frustration, anger or long-pent-up wrath. His response to these "people of Sodom and Gomorrah" is very different from the story related in the Book of Genesis the first time around. Every chance for reconciliation is given to them: whatever their sins are, however grave, God offers them purification, pardon and peace, if only they will turn back and walk with him again.

We ought to pay close attention here, and not only because it is the same forgiveness that the Lord offers to us, which ought to make us grateful and confident, and get us to the confessional. It is also the kind of mercy that he expects us to show to one another. We can excuse things that are excusable, but we are called to forgive things that are inexcusable, with love that wipes away the darkest stains of sin and heals the deepest wound. This love can only have its origin in God.

It is time to deal with *the weariness of* our *souls*, and to put down the terrible burden that is unforgiveness. The Lord offers us his limitless *forgiveness*, and will help us with his grace and *blessing* to extend his merciful love to others.

Wednesday of the Second Week of Lent

Bestow upon your servants, Lord,
abundance of grace and protection;
grant health of mind and body;
grant fullness of fraternal charity,
and make them always devoted to you.
Through Christ our Lord.

Jr 18:18-20; *Ps* 31; *Mt* 2:17-28

∞

Today's *Prayer over the People* asks a lot from the Lord, although they are fairly standard petitions. We ask the Lord to give us *abundance of grace and protection* - who could argue with that? Then *health of mind and body* - a very good idea as well, especially in this season of fasting and abstinence. We ask him to make us devoted to himself, to keep us close and to help us to love. All very good prayers. But there in the middle of the prayer, we ask the Lord to *grant fullness of fraternal charity*. Here is something different. We have been asking to receive all those good things from the Lord, but this petition is something we will have to use, to work at. It is not about getting, so much as giving.

It is important that we mention all of these petitions together, that we ask for love at the same time that we seek health and protection. For loving one another is essential to spiritual health and well-being, and the things that divide us are poison.

Consider the Gospel story: Jesus was with the apostles, and warned them of his impending Passion; he "took the Twelve to one side," Matthew tells us, to talk with them. Then the wife of Zebedee "came with her sons" to Jesus to make their request. When the rest of the Twelve reacted with jealousy, Jesus "called to them" again. Why all this movement? Hadn't they already been called aside together to talk with him?

Of course they had, but when Jesus predicted his Passion, the apostles' self-regard and anxiety moved them away from him. When they grumbled about the ambition of James and John, their own jealousy and unkindness broadened the distance between them. Sin is isolating: our selfish choices lead us away from Jesus, and away from one another. The plan of the Lord is to summon us away from sin, to call us to himself so that we can be healed.

Ultimately, all of our petitions are about doing and giving, not just getting. We ask the Lord for health, so that we can carry out his will with zeal and strength. We ask him for protection, so that we may persevere in the face of enemies and obstacles. And we ask him - we *must* ask him - for fraternal charity, so that, drawing close to others, we may find our way to Christ.

Thursday of the Second Week of Lent

Abide with your servants, O Lord,
who implore the help of your grace,
that they may receive from you
the support and guidance of your protection.
Through Christ our Lord.

Jr 17:5-10; *Ps* 1; *Lk* 16:19-31

∽

If anyone knows first-hand the truth of Jeremiah's words
- not to trust in human beings for help and support - it is
Lazarus, the poor man in today's Gospel. It seems that no
amount of begging, no appeal to human sympathy, would
be successful in approaching the rich man for help.

The rich man kept all of his goods for himself, and
he enjoyed himself very much, never needing to turn to
anyone else. He could trust in himself and his possessions.

How is it, then, that the situation of Lazarus and the
rich man seems so different from the results promised
by the Lord through the prophet? Lazarus trusts in the
Lord; the rich man trusts in himself and in material
things. Yet Lazarus is the one who ends up "parched",
like "dry scrub in the wasteland", in the midst of a dry
and "uninhabited land", while the rich man "has no

worries" as he relaxes in his luxurious home with every possible comfort around him.

It is easy to see that the tables will be turned, as Jesus himself affirms, in the next life, where we see Lazarus in paradise and the rich man in torment. There is, however, another aspect to the story that shows us how, even if outwardly the position of the two men seems to be incorrect, their real story, their true position, is clear to the Lord.

Consider how Jesus speaks of them. Everyone in the village would have known the name of the rich man, and would have used it frequently, to flatter or to beg. On the other hand, it doesn't seem that anyone paid much more attention to the poor man than the rich man himself did - he was one more nameless beggar to be walked around and ignored. Yet, when Jesus tells the story, it is Lazarus whom he calls by name, while the famous, wealthy citizen remains anonymous.

Our identity is founded on our relationship with God. Lazarus depended on God completely and was welcomed by name into paradise. The rich man, who never called on the name of the Lord, found himself distant from God in his moment of suffering, having lost everything he depended on - even his famous name.

We need the *help* of God's *grace* to be able to see past the superficial - to see what God sees, to understand his priorities and the way that he looks at us. When we ask for and receive such *guidance*, it changes our attitude and perspective. We can reach out to the poor with generous hearts, because we recognise God in each of them. We can depend on the Lord for our support, because he knows us and calls us by name.

Friday of the Second Week of Lent

Grant your people, O Lord, we pray,
health of mind and body,
that by constancy in good deeds
they may always merit the defence of your protection.
Through Christ our Lord.

    Gn 37:3-4,12-13a,17b-28a; *Ps* 105; *Mt* 21:33-43,45-46

∞

There is an awful lot of bad behaviour in today's readings!
That's an understatement, really: murder and the threat of
murder run all through them. And the readings seem to
have a strange attitude toward it. Take the First Reading:
the brothers of Joseph decide, in their jealousy, that they
want him out of the way. Then Reuben speaks up: let's not
kill him, let's just leave him to starve. And then Judah: let's
not kill him, let's sell him and let someone else do it. The
Gospel, too: here is the one who will inherit everything;
let's kill him and then the inheritance will come to us. As if
the vineyard owner would ever consider *that* a good idea.

Then again, consider the master's response in the
Gospel. As the Pharisees and scribes acknowledge, he is
coming to take care of things, but not just to punish the
murders and beatings. "He will bring those wretches to a

wretched end", of course, but this is not his only concern. Then he will "lease his vineyard to other tenants who will deliver the produce to him when the season arrives" - as Jesus confirms, "people who will produce fruit".

Here is the point of the Gospel - here is the heart of discipleship. We are called to bear fruit, to receive the Word of God and work with it, so that it has an effect on our lives, our words and our actions. When we are not living up to this, it causes problems in our relationship with God. Like the tenants, we avoid his messengers - we stop praying about certain parts of our lives, and stray away from the Word of God and the reminders and challenges it brings. In our defensiveness we may even turn to sins that make us feel better, but wound or even kill the life of Christ in our souls.

What we need, then, is a renewal of our desire to bear fruit, the grace of *constancy in good deeds* that is a daily response to the gifts that God has entrusted to us. By constancy, by perseverance, we stay close to him, and he gives us the best reward for our labour: a share of the fruit we have borne for him, and the constant *defence of* his *protection*.

Yes, the jealous, selfish people in the readings have some peculiar ideas, and do some terrible things. But the Lord will give us a clear, *healthy mind* to know his will. We must devote our strength to constancy in bearing good fruit.

Saturday of the Second Week of Lent

May the ears of your mercy be open, O Lord,
to the prayers of those who call upon you;
and that you may grant them what they desire,
have them ask what is pleasing to you.
Through Christ our Lord.

Mi 7:14-15,18-20; Ps 103; Lk 15:1-3,11-32

Even a person who would be hard-pressed to relate anything about the Gospel - who couldn't name a second parable of Jesus, who has never heard of the Sermon on the Mount - knows the story of the Prodigal Son. It seems, in many ways, the perfect parable. It has just enough drama to grab one's attention, enough generalities to allow the listener to fill in his own details - to imagine, like the older brother did, just how out of hand things became for the Prodigal (that is, the wasteful, careless, spendthrift) son.

More important, and more intriguing, is the wonderful drama of the son's return to find his father already looking for him. The father showers so much mercy, forgiveness and generosity on him, out of all proportion to what he really deserves, that we could just as easily call this parable the story of the Prodigal Father.

It is wonderful to contemplate such boundless forgiveness, to know that *the ears of* God's *mercy*, as the *Prayer over the People* puts it today, are always open to us when we need to be reconciled. But what about the times when we stand in the place of the older son, and find it difficult to forgive others?

The Lord makes it clear that, if we want a relationship with him, we must forgive others just as he forgives them. It is at the heart, not just of this parable, but of the *Our Father* as well. We know that the best way to learn forgiveness is to pray for the one who has hurt us - to move someone from our list of grievances to our list of intercessions. But the *Prayer over the People* teaches us that we have to do this in a particular way.

If we wish the ears of God's mercy to be open to us, if we want him to *grant what* we *desire*, then we must *ask* for *what is pleasing to* the Lord. How could our prayer not be pleasing to him? Suppose we say, for example, "Heal my relationship with *X*", while what we mean is "Make *X* see that he was wrong, and come and ask my forgiveness." Or we ask God to help *Y* to get back to Church and to change her ways, when our real motivation is that *Y's* behaviour is embarrassing to us, and we want it to stop.

Instead, we ought to pray asking God to do what he already wants to do: to reveal to each person exactly how much he loves him or her. That's it - no instructions for God, no timetable - but really that's everything. If a person knows how much he is loved, he will want to change. If we know how much we are loved, we can love and forgive others.

God sent his Son into the world to teach us how much we are loved, and how much he wishes to bestow mercy and reconciliation on all of his children. A prayer for a deeper knowledge of this essential truth, for ourselves and others, is a prayer that brings true healing, and a prayer to which the ears of God's mercy will always be open.

Third Sunday of Lent

Direct, O Lord, we pray, the hearts of your faithful,
and in your kindness grant your servants this grace:
that, abiding in the love of you and their neighbour,
they may fulfil the whole of your commands.
Through Christ our Lord.

> *Year A: Ex* 17:3-7; *Ps* 95; *Rm* 5:1-2,5-8; *Jn* 4:5-42
> *Year B: Ex* 20:1-17; *Ps* 19; *1 Co* 1:22-25; *Jn* 2:13-25
> *Year C: Ex* 3:1-8a,13-15; *Ps* 103; *1 Co* 10:1-6,10-12; *Lk* 13:1-9

∞

The *Prayer over the People* today once again calls us
to perfection in serving the Lord. *Direct, O Lord ... the*
hearts of your faithful ... that they may fulfil the whole
of your commands. Certainly it's a worthy petition: it is
Lent, after all, and we ought to be striving for greater
faithfulness and holiness. The whole point of these
special prayers is to ask God for strength and help as we
strive to do his will more perfectly.

A real blessing, though, is the way in which this prayer
focuses our attention on the source of this strength to
do God's will. We receive and increase the ability to do
good, it says, by *abiding in the love of God and of* our
neighbour. It is not willpower that is needed, nor a detailed

daily schedule, nor lots of books filled with advice. What we need most is to know that God loves us, and how God loves us. When we are convinced of that, then the love of God enables us to do great things.

Look at the woman of Samaria. Her sinful living situation had control of her life. John tells us that she went to the well at noon - in the heat of the day, when she could be sure that no one else would be there. Perhaps she made this choice to avoid the gossip and criticism of the villagers, who would have taunted her with her sins. When Jesus offers her living water, the gift of the Spirit and of eternal life, she is willing to miss out on this gift rather than converse honestly with him.

Yet, by the end of the story, she sets down her burden, runs to the people of the village, the people she had been avoiding for so long, and tells them of her newfound faith in "a man who has told me everything I ever did". Most of the people in the town probably told her everything she ever did, and told her on a daily basis! What is the difference here?

Jesus treated her with compassion, even as he expected an honest reckoning of her situation and invited her to conversion. He stayed with her when she would have pushed him away; he looked at her when she would have liked to stay hidden. He revealed his identity to her and expected her, trusted her, to respond in faith. He did not overlook her sins, but invited her to place them in the context of his merciful, redeeming love.

Writing to the Romans, Saint Paul makes sure that we realise just how wonderful it is that "while we were still sinners" Christ showed his love for us to the point of death. It is unheard of, really - no one would ever think of doing such a thing, even for an innocent person. But Christ has done it for us. He is well aware of our sins, and still he died for love of us. He knows when we are making excuses, and he died for love of us. He was with us even as we wandered, and he died for love of us. He knows the temptations we face, he knows how difficult we find it to accept his love, and still he died for love of us.

We may feel unworthy of his love - and we would be absolutely correct! We may find it difficult to accept, because we have not experienced such love before; because it seems to require so much from us; because we are not sure we want to change. Yet, while we are still sinners, Christ has shown his love for us, and remains close to us. We need to learn a lesson from the woman at the well: the Lord is not going anywhere, and he will not stop calling us until we know and accept his love.

Then, we must respond. We must put down the burden of our sins, and reach out with his love to those around us. Why avoid it? Because it seems difficult? Because the future is unknown? Still, we know this for certain: that the love of God for us has no limits, and the love of God for us makes us do great things.

Monday of the Third Week of Lent

May your right hand, we ask, O Lord,
protect this people that makes entreaty to you:
graciously purify them and give them instruction,
that, finding solace in this life,
they may reach the good things to come.
Through Christ our Lord.

2 K 5:1-15ab; Ps 42; Lk 4:24-30

∞

The *Prayer over the People* today asks God for two things to help us reach eternal life: purification and solace. The first is easy to see in the readings today, as we consider the healing of Naaman - one of the few Old Testament stories that the Lord Jesus refers to in his public ministry. Solace, on the other hand, is a bit more difficult to understand, though we will find that if we try to comprehend solace, it will tell us something important about purification.

Solace comes from the same root as *consolation*, and in many ways it is a shortened form of that important word. In turn, *consolation*, as Pope Benedict XVI explained in his encyclical on hope (*Spe Salvi*, 38), comes from the Latin *solus*, that is, "alone", with a prefix than means "together". We are able to console a person, the Holy Father explained, by being with him as he suffers - that is, by being with him at the moment when he is most alone. In so doing we take away the most potent form of suffering, isolation, and lighten the burden as we share it.

In the same way, we receive consolation from Christ by the reality of his Incarnation, when he took on our human nature in order to become "God with us". He accepted our weakness, to be with us when we are weak. He took on our poverty, to be with us to sustain us. He bore our pain, not just to save us from suffering, but in a mysterious way to save us through suffering. Even when our painful circumstances remain and must be borne, we know he is with us, and this gives us solace and strength.

So, when we look at healing in Scripture and in our own lives, we find that what is needed most is the faith to know that Christ is with us; the hope to entrust our needs to him; and the love to open our hearts to him and let him into our lives. Naaman found that healing does not come from worldly power, or require exciting, showy things. Rather, his healing came from a willingness to take the Lord at his word and trustingly obey him. Jesus could not work miracles in Nazareth because they would not do this - there was no room in their hearts for him. When they became defensive, there wasn't even room in their town for him.

As we approach Jesus for healing - from sin, from pain, from fear - we must remember that what he wants most of all is to be with us and to stay with us. He will purify, strengthen and heal us; he will show us that we are not alone. If we allow him, he will stay with us along our sometimes painful path, all the way to heaven.

Tuesday of the Third Week of Lent

O God, founder and ruler of your people,
drive away the sins that assail them,
that they may always be pleasing to you
and ever safe under your protection.
Through Christ our Lord.

Dn 3:25,34-43; *Ps* 25; *Mt* 19:21-35

∞

There are few things in life more intimidating, more
oppressive, than to be in debt. This is especially true
in a society that values its members by what they can
produce, by what they can do for themselves. It can be
a humiliating experience to have to admit that you are
unable to pay what you owe. It doesn't have to be a large
debt, either; just enough to be beyond your own ability.
Whenever we have to ask someone for help, we expose
ourselves to questions and criticism: "How could you
spend so much? What were you thinking? Why weren't
you more careful?" And often the assistance that is given
to get us out of debt comes with strings attached - high
interest rates; a probationary period; requirements that
someone else approve future transactions. Perhaps this
is why it can be so easy to get deeper into debt: it seems

less difficult to try to fix it yourself than to ask someone else for help.

With the Lord there is none of this, however. When we turn back to him - and this Lent is precisely that: a time for turning back - when we ask him to *drive away the sins that assail us*, he does not hold it over our heads, demanding excuses and explanations. Instead, when we admit our guilt and ask for forgiveness, he bestows his mercy in abundance, out of proportion to our deserving it, and with no conditions other than a commitment to try to sin no more.

Just how abundant is God's mercy? In the Gospel, Jesus mentions two debts: one which a servant owes his master, and another that is owed to him by a fellow servant. Jesus uses Greek units of currency which are based on the daily wage of an unskilled labourer. The fellow servant owes our protagonist a hundred *denarii*, that is, a hundred days' wages. A modern equivalent works out to about £6,000 - not a negligible debt, but one that could be managed with time and discipline. On the other hand, the servant owed the master 10,000 talents, and a talent was equivalent to 10,000 *denarii*. He owed his master a million times the amount that he was owed - £6 billion, larger than the national debt of some sovereign countries! There was no way that he would ever be able to pay back such a sum.

How does his master respond when the servant begs for mercy? He "cancelled the debt". That's it - no demand for explanation, no strings attached. The master simply gives an impossibly huge measure of forgiveness, doing for the servant what he could never do for himself. Faced with such extraordinary love, he should have responded to his fellow servant with generosity and mercy. Because he refused to be merciful in turn, he lost his own chance for forgiveness.

Having received such wondrous love from the Lord, how can we ever hold our brothers and sisters to a different standard? Our sins against the *founder and ruler* of the People of God are surely more serious than any injury or debt we might hold against another. When we recognise the abundance of God's limitless mercy, we must go and do likewise, loving and forgiving each other from the heart.

Wednesday of the Third Week of Lent

Give to your people, our God,
a resolve that is pleasing to you,
for, by conforming them to your teachings,
you bestow on them every favour.
Through Christ our Lord.

Dt 4:1,5-9; *Ps* 147; *Mt* 5:17-19

∽

Both of today's readings speak about the commandments of the Lord - and rightly so, since our Lenten sacrifices and discipline, especially our Lenten reflection and prayer, are meant to assist us to purify our minds and change our actions to be more responsive to the Lord's commandments, to be *conformed to* his *teachings*. The readings set a high bar for us to reach: "Take care what you do and be on your guard …" "Keep and observe [the commandments] …" "Not one little stroke … will pass away." "The man who infringes even one of the least of these commandments … will be called least." When there are high expectations on us, there is a choice we must make: whether to live up to them, or to bristle at the fact that we have to obey, and get defensive, testy and even resentful at God's expectations on us.

Moses gives us the best reason to follow the Law of the Lord and to keep the commandments. Far from being an imposition on us, he insists, the commands of the Lord are a gift, and a sign of God's love. "What great nation is there that has its gods so near as the Lord our God is to us? … And what great nation is there that has laws and customs to match this whole Law?" The pagan gods were capricious, a source of anxiety and fear because no one ever knew what they wanted or what they would do next. Pagan sacrifices served to placate the gods, to buy their good behaviour for a little while longer. The Lord God, Moses explains, makes his will known to us explicitly, consistently. In his love for us he marks out the way that leads us to him, and in doing so he *bestows* his *favour* on us.

This must ultimately be our motivation for keeping the Law: that the commands of the Law are the rules of our relationship with God. Every relationship has rules, after all, and the obligations we have are loving responses to the love we have received from God. Moses wants the people to remember not just what God has said, but what he did throughout all those years in the desert. Jesus wants us to keep in mind what we have heard from God, and what he did to fulfil his Word. Then every good deed will be a response to the One who has been so good to us. The commandments will become, not a means of oppression, or a reason for resentment, but a daily opportunity to make acts of love.

Thursday of the Third Week of Lent

We call on your loving kindness
and trust in your mercy, O Lord,
that, since we have from you all that we are,
through your grace we may seek what is right
and have strength to do the good we desire.
Through Christ our Lord.

Jr 7:23-28; *Ps* 95; *Lk* 11:14-23

∞

"If it is through the finger of God that I cast out devils, then know that the kingdom of God has overtaken you." The finger of God - what a curious expression! It is, of course, one of the traditional titles of the Holy Spirit: the hymn *Veni, Creator Spiritus* calls him *digitus paternae dexterae*, "finger of the Father's right hand". It may seem a bit below the dignity of the Third Person of the Most Holy Trinity, but actually it is quite an evocative image.

A finger points the way, after all. We use our fingers to make and shape things, especially those requiring fine details. A most intimate way of touching another person is with the fingertips. And a finger can poke when necessary, to get someone moving. Thus by using the image of the finger of God, Jesus is challenging us to recognise the presence of the Holy Spirit in our midst, and to acknowledge his power and action in our lives.

We need the Holy Spirit if we are going to overcome sinful habits and find *the strength to do the good* we *desire*. This is the petition we make at the end of the *Prayer over the People*, and the rest of the prayer shows us how to find this strength. "*We call on you … we trust you … we have from you all that we are*" - all of these statements express our trust in God, a trust that is based on experience of his action in our lives. This experience leads us to respond to him with faith and hope.

This is the constant theme of the Scriptures, especially the prophets: remember what God has done, and respond by staying close to him. This is the Lord's critique in the First Reading: the people are unfaithful and they do not remember. He brought them out of Egypt, and they went their own way. He sent them the prophets, and they pretended not to hear. He is sending them Jeremiah, and they will refuse to listen to him. Their unfaithfulness stems from the fact that they will not see what the Lord is doing for them.

It cannot be like that for us. We must recognise the work of the Holy Spirit - the finger of God's wisdom, strength and healing touch - and respond in word and action. The Spirit will point the way, and we must follow it. He will cast out sin and heal us, and we must make a lasting change. He will poke us, if he has to, to get us moving. We must get up and walk the way that leads to the Kingdom of God.

Friday of the Third Week of Lent

Look graciously, O Lord,
upon the faithful who implore your mercy,
that, trusting in your kindness,
they may spread far and wide
the gifts your charity has bestowed.
Through Christ our Lord.

Ho 14:2-10; *Ps* 81; *Mk* 12:28-34

In the Gospel reading, Our Lord seems impressed with the scribe who is able to make an important connection with what Jesus has said. "To love God ... and to love your neighbour ... is far more important than any holocaust or sacrifice." We ought to remember that the scribe was probably also a Pharisee, and the scribes and Pharisees were very concerned with making proper holocausts and sacrifices according to the Law of Moses. It is perhaps even more impressive, then, to hear this particular man conceding this specific point.

The reason he says it, though, is not because he has suddenly changed his mind about the need for offering sacrifices. Rather, he sees the important truth that loving this way is a sacrifice. To give one's whole mind, heart, soul and strength to the love of God is not some romantically pious notion. No: if we love God daily, we must daily offer up and hand over our whole selves. We need to offer our minds, so that his priorities come before our own. We must give our hearts, so that we put him first before every other relationship and desire. We must hand over our soul and spirit, so that we may do his will cheerfully, not begrudgingly. We must devote to him all of our bodily strength, so that we may persevere in the face of fatigue and overcome selfish desires.

We mustn't deceive ourselves about just how many personal sacrifices will be involved in *spreading far and wide the gifts* we have received from God's *charity*, putting them into action in love of neighbour. It is a sacrifice to try to see things from someone else's perspective, to put another's needs before our own. It can be difficult to act at all times with sincerity and generosity of spirit, to love readily, perseveringly, patiently, tirelessly. All of this requires a daily dying to self, a daily self-sacrifice on the altar of God's love.

Just as in the Temple those who brought a sacrifice to the Lord were given some of it back to be their food, when we offer ourselves - mind, heart, spirit and body - to the Lord, he purifies and strengthens the gifts we make, and gives them back to us enlivened and renewed. This is how we are able to love him and to spread his love far and wide. Because we have been transformed by his gifts of charity, his perfect love, we can make a total offering of ourselves to him and to others.

Saturday of the Third Week of Lent

Hold out to your faithful people, Lord,
the right hand of heavenly assistance,
that they may seek you with all their heart
and merit the granting of what they ask.
Through Christ our Lord.

Ho 6:1-6; *Ps* 51; *Lk* 18:9-14

∞

Jesus tells us in today's Gospel that the tax collector "went home again at rights with God" and that the Pharisee did not. Some translations say that he went home "justified", but we need to make sure that we understand this term. We are not talking about "feeling justified", that is, having a rationale for our behaviour or decisions, or being convinced that we are in the right. If that were the case, then the Pharisee, smug as he is, would be the one who was "justified". Rather, in the New Testament, justification - literally, "making just" - is the term that describes what God does when he makes us like himself in the redemption won by Christ. He reorients our lives, reunites us to himself, and recreates the bond between us that enables us to live holy lives because we are living like him and with him. In this sense we could just as easily call it *deification* - that is, making us like God - for to be holy is to be like the Holy One.

Why does only one man in the story find justification? The Pharisee, after all, does many just and holy things, as he himself notes! But there is the first symptom - Jesus tells us that "he said this prayer to himself". Of course, talking to oneself is no prayer at all. The Pharisee may be striving to do good works, but he is not trying to be like God. He doesn't act like God: he despises everyone who does not live up to his standards. He doesn't help like God: he sees a sinner and he closes his mind and heart to him. He doesn't love like God: he is so turned in on himself that even in the Temple he cannot really be present to God or neighbour.

The tax collector, on the other hand, knows his weakness. More importantly, he knows where to turn for help. Because his heart is broken with shame and sorrow, he can *seek* the Lord *with all* his *heart*. Because his sins have isolated him from others, he can reach out with hope and joy to grace, the *right hand of heavenly assistance* that the Lord *holds out* to him. Because he knows how much he needs the Lord, he can trust God to *grant what* he *asks*.

It is this trust that leads to a relationship with the Lord, the right relationship of justification. When we recognise our need for God, and how he responds to our needs, then we can respond to him by staying close and striving to live like him. Otherwise we run the risk of talking only to ourselves, instead of addressing the One who can make us who we ought to be.

Fourth Sunday of Lent

Look upon those who call to you, O Lord,
and sustain the weak;
give life by your unfailing light
to those who walk in the shadow of death,
and bring those rescued by your mercy from every evil
to reach the highest good.
Through Christ our Lord.

Year A: 1 S 16:1b,6-7,10-13a; *Ps* 23; *Ep* 5:8-14; *Jn* 9:1-41
Year B: 2 Ch 36:14-16,19-23; *Ps* 137; *Ep* 2:4-10; *Jn* 3:14-21
Year C: Jos 5:9a,10-12; *Ps* 34; *2 Co* 5:17-21; *Lk* 15:1-3,11-32

∞

Imagine what it must have been like for the man born blind suddenly to be able to see. Never mind: it is not possible for us to imagine. Sight is something we take for granted: from the moment we were born, we have never had to say, "I am going to see now; how do I go about it?" It is one of the most automatic things we do. We can make a deliberate decision *not* to see - we can close our eyes tight and refuse to open them - but for most of our lives the only thing we need do in order to see is to be alive and healthy.

Not so for the man born blind. He hadn't lost his sight and now regained it; he had no idea what it was like to see.

When Jesus healed him, it was as if he had become a new person. All of a sudden he had an extra sense. He interacted with the world and received information from it in a way he had never done before. He had to think about and communicate about things he had never considered before: colour, for a start; brightness; facial expressions and body language, and all sorts of non-verbal communications; clouds, the sun and moon, the stars. He was, without an ounce of exaggeration, a new person, a man reborn. It must have filled him with intense joy, and terrified him at the same time.

We always read this Gospel on the Fourth Sunday of Lent at Masses where there are catechumens present, those who are preparing to be baptised at the Easter Vigil. It is chosen to introduce the theme of enlightenment - of receiving the Light of Christ, the light of faith, in Baptism. The particular situation of the man born blind teaches us that God grants new *life by* his gift of the *unfailing light* of faith. This enlightenment is meant to transform the baptised, to make us new people, with a new way of encountering the world and making judgements about it. This light gives us a new perspective, a new ability to see the beauty of goodness and the horror of sin. It allows us to see Christ present in our midst, and the path that he has marked out for us.

When we are seeing clearly, and keeping our eyes on Christ, we have a new ability to respond to him with courage, with confidence, even with boldness. Consider the man born blind: this humble beggar, all of a sudden, is able to confront the Sanhedrin and the mockery of the scribes and Pharisees. They are not quite pleased with the theology lesson he provides them, but he says it anyway. He doesn't quibble or argue with them, but simply states what he knows: I was blind, now I see. The man who did this to me must be something special.

Our enlightenment by Christ gives us strength to confront an even more intimidating adversary. The *Prayer over the People* asks the Lord to *rescue* us *from every evil*, by shining his light on those *who walk in the shadow of death*. Why do we sin? Usually because the fear of death - and of all the little, daily deaths like being left out, not being loved, having to sacrifice - leads us to trust ourselves rather than God. The light of Christ exposes the lies of the Evil One. It shows us the glory of the Resurrection, which follows every freely accepted cross. It reveals God as the source of grace and strength that *sustains the weak*. It empowers us to reject the Great Lie that says that God cannot be trusted, and to follow Christ in faith in order *to reach the highest good*.

The light of Christ gives us new life - a new kind of life, a new way of seeing life. What a tragedy it would be if we closed our eyes to this miracle. What a difference it makes when we keep our eyes fixed on Christ.

Monday of the Fourth Week of Lent

Renew your people within and without, O Lord,
and, since it is your will
that they be unhindered by bodily delights,
give them, we pray,
perseverance in their spiritual intent.
Through Christ our Lord.

Is 65:17-21; *Ps* 30; *Jn* 4:43-54

∞

What a treasure we have in the Most Blessed Sacrament, which is the way in which the Lord *renews* his *people within and without*, as the *Prayer over the People* assures us. The Lord gives himself to us to be our food, to be one with us in body as well as in spirit. By his presence he can heal and transform us from the inside out, as it were. He can put the delights of the body in proper perspective, and help us to make sacrifices to train the senses and desires to be submissive to the guidance of the soul. He gives us strength to persevere in penance and offerings, even when we really want the sweets, or the coffee, or whatever else it is that we have given up for love of him.

He is the source of our strength: as he will say soon after this passage in John's Gospel, his flesh is real food for us, and we need to receive him if we are to survive. So why don't we ask him for strength and help all the time? Perhaps it is too easy to suppose that he is not interested - that our hunger or cravings or emotional attachments are somehow too mundane, too ordinary to tell him. Or perhaps we think that it would be better to try to handle things ourselves, by sheer willpower. Perhaps we are attached to our *bodily delights* and not quite ready to give them up.

In these cases, we need to run to Jesus, who makes himself little in the Blessed Sacrament because he is concerned with all the little details of our lives. We need to have the attitude of the royal official in the Gospel, who was tested by Jesus, for his own sake and for ours. He teaches us to pray with confidence - Lord, come now to help, or my child will die. When we need the Lord's help, there is no time to waste. Only he can help us. Only he can heal us. Only he can strengthen us.

Whenever we turn to him - in the moment of temptation; as we are opening the cupboard or the refrigerator; at the very moment we are reaching out for that bodily delight - whenever we ask for his grace, it is "exactly the time" that he gives us the strength we need for *perseverance in* our *spiritual intent*. He *renews us within and without* by his saving presence, and by his abundant love.

Tuesday of the Fourth Week of Lent

Grant, O merciful God,
that your people may remain always devoted to you
and may constantly receive from your kindness
whatever is for their good.
Through Christ our Lord.

Ezk 47:1-9,12; *Ps* 46; *Jn* 5:1-16

∽

The *Prayer over the People* for today's Mass focuses our attention on the idea of constancy and perseverance. It uses words like *remain; always devoted; constantly;* and asks God to give us *whatever is for* our *good*, in any set of circumstances. It reflects for us the proper response to the attitude of generosity that God shows to us, which we see in Ezekiel's vision in the First Reading. When we are told that the trees beside the river of God bear leaves and fruit in every season, it means that they are always accessible to whoever needs their saving properties.

The Gospel speaks of a different kind of permanence, however. The paralysed man, we are told, had been lame for thirty-eight years - for most, if not all, of his life. It seems from the story that he was a "regular" at the Pool of Bethesda; perhaps he even lived in its porticoes year-round. Even if he had only started going to the pool when he became an adult, that's twenty years and more of being near the water with no success.

What is his explanation? Every time I try to get to the pool, he says, someone else gets there ahead of me. For twenty years? In all that time, he never picked a different spot? Never tried to get closer? Never tried to work it out with other "regulars" to let him give it a try? In all of that time of waiting and watching, he never tried to change his routine? We can understand, perhaps, why Jesus asks him if he really wants to be well.

When the paralysed man confides his need and desire to Christ, his healing is complete and immediate. He teaches us several lessons. One is how easy it can be to get into habits of thinking and acting - habits of sin - that may seem small but have a paralysing effect on us. Acknowledging the problem is only a beginning, though: it requires courage and creativity to get the help we need and to put it into practice. Moreover, when we approach Jesus for help, he is going to ask us if we really want to be well, if we are ready to let go and to make a change.

His grace will help us to do this. His grace is constant and sure, and when we are healed by it, we must respond with constancy and not sin any more. If Christ has healed us and set us free, we must walk the way with him, and never return to the place in which we were stuck, paralysed by our sins.

Wednesday of the Fourth Week of Lent

May your servants be shielded, O Lord,
by the protection of your loving-kindness,
that, doing what is good in this world,
they may reach you, their highest good.
Through Christ our Lord.

Is 49:8-15; *Ps* 145; *Jn* 5:17-30

∞

Both of the readings today speak about the end of time
- or, more specifically, the time *after* the end. The Lord
speaks through Isaiah, and promises restoration, health
and comfort, nourishment and light to those who fear the
Lord - all the *loving kindness* we pray for in the *Prayer
over the People*. Jesus speaks about the resurrection of
the dead, and of their judgement according to their deeds
- which is why the prayer acknowledges that we *reach* our
highest good by *doing what is good in this world* with the
help of God's grace.

The question is whether these two descriptions are
mutually exclusive, opposed to one another, whether
the loving kindness of God is incompatible with his just
judgement. Intellectually, theologically, we know the right
answer - of course they go together. But it doesn't always

feel that way, so we should be clear about the connection between mercy and judgement.

"He who pities them will lead them," Isaiah says, "and guide them to springs of water." These lines, and the reference a few verses before about pastures, remind us that here we are encountering the Good Shepherd, who gathers and leads his people. It is one of the tenderest images in all the Scripture, full of loving kindness, especially here, when the Shepherd promises never to forget his flock.

If we are going to belong to the flock, though, one thing is essential: we must follow the Shepherd. The judgement that the Lord will pass on his flock will not be based on some external, mechanical law, but on the question of whether we have stayed close to him, listened to him, followed him. Why is it that Jesus will do the judging? Because he has set us an example: "The Son can do nothing by himself," he says, "he can do only what he sees the Father doing." He follows perfectly the will of the Father. If we want to belong to him, if we want to receive his loving kindness, we must listen for his voice and follow his example.

Lent is a time for us to listen again to the voice of the Lord. Our Good Shepherd helps and shields us; he gives us his loving kindness and strength for *doing what is good*. In return, he asks for no more, but certainly no less, than that we should follow him.

Thursday of the Fourth Week of Lent

O God, protector of all who hope in you,
bless your people, keep them safe,
defend them, prepare them,
that, free from sin and safe from the enemy,
they may persevere always in your love.
Through Christ our Lord.

Ex 32:7-14; *Ps* 106; *Jn* 5:31-47

∞

After all that the Israelites had been through, on their way out of Egypt and to Mount Sinai, it seems inconceivable that they would arrive at the tragedy of the Golden Calf. How quickly they turned away from the Lord, and to depths of depravity that had not been heard of before! The Book of Exodus gives us insight into their rationale: Moses had been gone for weeks at the top of the mountain; they said they didn't know when, or if, he would return. They were getting scared, and they wanted something tangible to comfort themselves. So they made a god like the Egyptians had - an idol that they could see and touch, a visible focus for their anxieties and their needs.

The terrible argument between God and Moses at the top of the mountain shows us how wrong the people were.

"Go down … [to] your people," the Lord tells Moses, "whom you brought out of Egypt." Moses does not let this characterisation go unchallenged: he knows the truth, and he teaches it to us. The Israelites are not *his* people; he has not brought them out of slavery by himself. The Lord rescued his own "people … with arm outstretched and mighty hand". Even if all the people had forgotten, Moses remembered what the Lord had done, and he pleaded with him to do it again. He knew that the works of the Lord were proof of his protection - tangible, visible proof of his love, if only the Israelites would open their eyes to see. The works of the Lord should have been their reason for trusting him.

Jesus tells us the same thing: that if we want to know who he is, and why we should believe in him, the works that he performs will show us. The *Prayer over the People* today asks him to do quite a few of these works: to *bless* his *people, keep them safe, defend them* and set them *free from sin and safe from the enemy*. We put our trust in the Lord and know that he will answer our needs. But there is more than that. The works that he does are meant also to *prepare* us and to give us the strength to *persevere always in* his *love*.

Preparation is the watchword for the season of Lent. Many in the Church are in their final stage of purification and preparation for receiving the Sacraments of Initiation at Easter. The rest of us are preparing to renew our

Baptismal promises, the commitment we made to the Lord when he gave his life to us, and asked us for our whole life in return. It is an act of faith to give ourselves completely to the Lord, and to reject everything that is not from him. But our faith is not blind. As we pay attention to his works of love and mercy - in history, in our own lives - we find the tangible, visible assurance we need to be able to trust him, to follow him, to persevere in his service.

Friday of the Fourth Week of Lent

Look upon your servants, O Lord,
and in your goodness protect with heavenly assistance
those who trust in your mercy.
Through Christ our Lord.

Ws 2:1a,12-22; Ps 34; Jn 7:1-2,10,25-30

∽

Today we continue reading the account of the controversies developing between Jesus and the Pharisees - controversies that eventually lead to his trial and his being handed over to death. Once again the leaders of the people get very angry with Jesus, and even try to arrest him, because he speaks of his unique relationship with God the Father in terms that sound to them like blasphemy, a denial of their faith in the One God.

Beyond the charge of blasphemy, though, perhaps we can hear other things as well. Jealousy? Defensiveness? An unwillingness to change? We hear it in the First Reading, too: speaking about the just man, the people say, "He claims to have knowledge of God, and calls himself a son of the Lord. The very sight of him weighs our spirits down; his way of life is not like that of others."

How do they try to avoid facing the fact of Jesus' true identity? By categorising him - putting him in a little box

that makes him just like everyone else. They say they have him figured out - we know who he is. We know where he's from, and so he can't be anyone important. He certainly can't be the Messiah.

It is significant that this encounter happened during the Feast of Tabernacles. The Jews talked about Jesus' hometown, his house. But during the feast, everyone came to Jerusalem and lived in huts specially constructed for the occasion. It was meant to remind them of the days of desert wandering, when their ancestors did not have a permanent home, but lived in tents, followed the pillar of cloud, and relied completely upon the Lord to *look upon* his *servants* and *protect* them *with heavenly assistance*. The people needed to be reminded that this world is passing, and that they were pilgrims passing through. They had to learn not to cling to anything temporary, not even their own opinions of what God could or should do. They needed to know that their true home was Heaven, and that Christ came from there in order to take them back with him.

We also have a choice to make: will we construct immovable spiritual edifices, put walls around our intellect and our will? Or will we depend totally on God, and respond generously to him - moving when he moves us, adjusting our thoughts and actions to the commands of his Word? If we *trust in his mercy* we have nothing to fear. We can follow him with confidence as he leads us to our true, lasting home.

Saturday of the Fourth Week of Lent

Look upon your people, O Lord,
and, as they draw near to the coming festivities,
bestow upon them abundance of heavenly grace,
that, helped by the consolations of this world,
they may be impelled more readily
towards higher goods that cannot be seen.
Through Christ our Lord.

Jr 11:18-20; *Ps* 7; *Jn* 7:40-53

∞

The fourth week of Lent ends as it began - at least as far as the *Prayer over the People* is concerned. Last Sunday we had a brief respite from the sadness and penance of Lent. Even the priest's rose-coloured vestments spoke of joy in the midst of sacrifice. Today's prayer is even bolder, in its way. It reminds us that we have to see the days of Holy Week as the *coming festivities*.

Does this make sense? How can the commemoration of the Passion, Death and burial of Christ be considered festive? It is not a new question, really. After all, faith invites us to consider how the day of the crucifixion, perhaps the worst day in the history of mankind, can be called *Good* Friday. And what about the rest of the prayer, which suggests that *the consolations of this world* should be a help towards the *higher goods* of heaven? Haven't we spent the last four weeks trying to avoid worldly consolations, and to fix our eyes on God alone?

The key to understanding how Lent and Holy Week can be festive and consoling lies in the perspective of faith. It teaches us to keep our eyes open to what God is doing, which always exceeds our expectations. It is the perspective that, sadly, led to division in the crowd outside the Temple, and in the council gathered within, as some people took the chance to consider that maybe they didn't know everything there was to know about Jesus. Perhaps there was more to the story than what they thought they had figured out. Perhaps, if they took what they saw and heard seriously, they could see God at work, and recognise the Messiah in their midst.

This is how we can greet both sorrow and consolation in this world, and make use of both in our striving towards the Lord. When we listen to God's perspective on these things - holding it above the opinions of others, and even our own preconceived notions - we see the hidden depth of God's plan. His plan makes even suffering into something worthy and meaningful, and transforms our daily experiences so that they lead us to him.

Fifth Sunday of Lent

Bless, O Lord, your people,
who long for the gift of your mercy,
and grant that what, at your prompting, they desire
they may receive by your generous gift.
Through Christ our Lord.

> *Year A: Ezk* 37:12-14; *Ps* 130; *Rm* 8:8-11; *Jn* 11:1-45
> *Year B: Jr* 31:31-34; *Ps* 51; *Heb* 5:7-9; *Jn* 12:20-33
> *Year C: Is* 43:16-21; *Ps* 126; *Ph* 3:8-14; *Jn* 8:1-11

∽

Do we really *long for the gift of* God's *mercy*? That is what
this season of Lent is about after all. The readings, the
hymns, the penance we perform, everything is meant to
convince us and enable us to turn again to the Lord and be
healed of sin. And the *Prayer over the People* today takes
it for granted that this is what we want. Because it is *at* the
Lord's *prompting* that we *desire* his love, we can ask for it
with confidence.

   How should we ask? There is a lesson to be learnt from
Martha, who turns to Jesus in her grief at her brother's
death. "Lord, if you had been here, my brother would not
have died," she says, and we need not view this scene like
a pious oil painting or stained glass window, but rather

give it all the emotion of a person who has just suffered the loss of a sibling.

"Even now," she goes on, "I know that whatever you ask of God, he will grant you." What an extraordinary act of faith, coming as it does in the midst of grief. Jesus asks to see the tomb; they go there together, and he orders that it be opened. Here Martha hesitates - "Lord, by now he will smell." All of a sudden, worldly concerns rush back into her heart, and threaten to replace faith with fear: of offending, of embarrassment. Hadn't she just acknowledged that Jesus could do what she was asking? Why should she hesitate now?

Saint Paul's teaching on the Resurrection in today's second reading tips us off that there is more to the story of the Raising of Lazarus than only what waits for us at death. Rather, each time that we receive the Lord's mercy - especially in the Sacrament of Confession - we experience a spiritual resurrection in our souls. The Lord raises us up from the death of sin to new life in the Holy Spirit. Like Martha, we know this intellectually; with the heart and the conscience we accept it as true and know that we ought to act. Why, then, are we hesitant to approach him?

Perhaps it has been a long time - and sin stinks. We know how to ask for mercy for small sins. But we need to be on our guard against rolling a stone across long-term habits, against deciding that it is too late to change, or too difficult, or that we'd rather not. It is precisely to these walled-off, sealed-up parts of the mind and heart that Jesus wants to go. He prompts us - he commands us - to roll away the stone and to let him in. Once we do, he raises us up, unties and untangles the attachments that we have to sin, and lets us go free.

Where do we find the courage to roll back the stone? In the same place that Martha found it. "Do you believe this?" Jesus asked, and she professes her faith in him. From the Greek verb that John chooses, as well as from the rest of Martha's story, we understand that her faith comes from experience. She has welcomed Jesus into her home, into her family. From watching him, from listening to him, she understands who he is and what he has come to do. The time she spent with Jesus led her to trust him, and enabled her to do what he asked.

It may often feel like too big a risk to roll back the stone for Christ. But when we risk it, we gain experience. We know more and more fully the generous gift of God's mercy. We entrust ourselves to him with hope and confidence, and experience the glory of each little resurrection.

Monday of the Fifth Week of Lent

Set free from their sins, O Lord, we pray,
the people who call upon you,
that, living a holy life,
they may be kept safe from every trial.
Through Christ our Lord.

Dn 13:1-62; *Ps* 23; *Jn* 8:1-11

☙

The readings today present similar stories: women accused of adultery, brought into the public square for trial and judgement, each of them saved by a last-moment intervention by the Lord. But we ought to look closely at the difference between the stories, which teaches us about the paradox of God's mercy.

The story of Susanna is a tragic one, not only because of the dreadful punishment that her accusers prepared for her, but because the story makes it clear that it is *so* unjust, that she is *so* innocent and pure of heart, willing to die rather than to offend the Lord. We, like the crowd, give thanks to God that he heard her plea and saw her plight, and sent his prophet to rescue her.

In the Gospel story, however, there is no helpless ingénue, but someone discovered in the very act of adultery. We can wonder why the elders brought only her to be judged, and let the man get away, but the fact remains that even she does not contest the reality of the sin.

Here we see the depths of God's mercy: in the face of her sinfulness, he does not condemn, does not ask for explanations, but simply forgives her wholeheartedly, and expects others to do the same. This is the paradox of which Saint Paul speaks in another place: it would be understandable for Jesus to protect the innocent, but the greatness of his love is demonstrated by the fact that he died for us "while we were still sinners" (*Rm* 5:8).

We must learn to act like this: to forgive from the heart even in the very face of an injury or an offence. We can do this if we are mindful of just how much we stand in need of forgiveness from God, and from others. We can be merciful if - and only if - we keep in mind how rich God's mercy has been to us.

After all, it is only because God is merciful that we are here. As the *Prayer over the People* reminds us, God *sets us free from* our *sins* so that we are able to live *a holy way of life*. His love, the initiative of his grace, comes first, and enables us to love others and to be merciful. Let us *call upon* him and ask him to *keep us safe*, to *set us free*, and to teach us to love as he does.

Tuesday of the Fifth Week of Lent

O God, who choose to show mercy not anger
to those who hope in you,
grant that your faithful may weep, as they should,
for the evil they have done,
and so merit the grace of your consolation.
Through Christ our Lord.

Nb 21:4-9; *Ps* 102; *Jn* 8:21-30

The wilderness in which the Israelites wandered for so many years was surely filled with all sorts of wild beasts, not least of which were the fiery serpents described in today's First Reading. ("Fiery" here probably refers to the poison bite of these snakes.) For decades now, the Lord has protected his people from all the dangers that surround them, but they complain - not for the first time - that they are tired of the provisions the Lord is making for them. So he seems to withdraw his protection for a while, allowing the serpents to afflict the people, and teaches them what it is like to have to survive on their own without him.

When the people finally cry out to the Lord, the remedy he prescribes is significant. By commanding Moses to make and mount a bronze serpent, the Lord reminds his people that he knows their needs and their afflictions. Moreover, he asserts his power, which far surpasses anything that could harm or attack his people.

The bronze serpent on the pole foreshadows, of course, the crucifixion of Jesus, as he himself makes clear in the Gospel. He has already told Nicodemus that he had to be lifted up, "as Moses lifted up the serpent in the desert" (*Jn* 3:14). Here, he foretells that all will behold him lifted up, and in seeing him will come to understand just who he is, and what he has come to do.

The *Prayer over the People* reminds us of our Lenten penances; it asks God to help us to *weep, as* we *should, for the evil* we *have done*. But our sorrow for sin is not an end in itself, and we should not become paralysed by guilt and shame. Repentance - true sorrow for sin combined with a firm commitment to change our lives - leads to *consolation*, which can only come from the Crucified Christ. When we see him lifted up, we realise that he has done this for love of us, sinners though we are. In his apparent defeat on the cross, we recognise his real power, the power of love that is stronger than any sin. He takes on our weakness - he takes our sins on his own shoulders - to prove that he knows our needs, he understands our struggles and our pain, and he is able to conquer all of it.

On the cross, Jesus reveals his plan for dealing once and for all with sin. We can be like the Israelites in the desert, and like the Pharisees in the Gospel, and try to solve our own problems and run our own lives. Or, we can place our lives in the outstretched hands of the One who comes to save us, who *shows mercy, not anger* and calls us to *hope in* him.

Wednesday of the Fifth Week of Lent

Attend, almighty God,
to the prayers of your people,
and, as you endow them
with confident hope in your compassion,
let them feel as ever the effects of your mercy.
Through Christ our Lord.

Dn 3:14-20,91-92,95; Dn 3:52-56; Jn 8:31-42

∞

There is some irony in the juxtaposition of today's two readings, and an opportunity for us to learn from the stubbornness of the disciples. Remember, the people who are arguing with Jesus are those "who believed in him", according to John. They followed him and had been attentive to his word, until he speaks of being set free. This they don't need, they insist: "We are descended from Abraham and we have never been the slaves of anyone."

The First Reading shows that these disciples must have contracted spiritual amnesia! Shadrach, Meshach and Abednego underwent their ordeal in Babylon - after Nebuchadnezzar had conquered Judah, enslaved the people, and forcibly removed them more than five hundred miles, from their homeland to his. Since those days, for five centuries by the time of the Lord, they had been occupied by foreign governments, most recently the Roman Empire. This is not even to mention the defining moment in their history as a people: the Exodus that took place after four centuries of exile and slavery in Egypt.

What a shame it is that they have put these events out of their minds. For it is in the context of such difficult events that we can often see most clearly the Lord *attend to the prayers of* his *people*, as he hears their cries and comes to save them. Because these disciples will not recall the things God has done in the past, they cannot recognise the saving mission of Jesus in their own day. Because they will not admit that they need saving, they cannot welcome the Saviour.

The *Prayer over the People* asks God to *endow* us *with confident hope in* his *compassion*, so that we can experience and *feel … the effects of* his *mercy*. In many ways, hope is a virtue of the memory, as we recall our need for God, and recognise his generous response to our needs. Hope enables us to recognise our weakness, our need to be saved and set free from sin, and to move trustingly toward the One who saves us. Denial of our weakness - spiritual amnesia, as it were - leaves us defensive, proud and very much on our own. If, on the other hand, we can entrust our needs to the God who always attends to our prayers, we can be set free by the truth of his love.

Thursday of the Fifth Week of Lent

Be gracious to your people, Lord, we pray,
that, as from day to day they reject what does not
*   please you,*
they may be filled instead with delight
*   at your commands.*
Through Christ our Lord.

Gn 17:3-9; Ps 105; Jn 8:51-59

∞

As contracts go, the covenant that God made with Abraham was a simple one. It comprises just six sentences. It could, perhaps, have been even a little shorter than that, as those six sentences repeat essentially the same thing over and over. In those *six sentences*, God mentions Abraham's fatherhood or his descendants *nine times*. In fact, he speaks of little else, except to make promises to be with those descendants, to care for them, to be their God.

So, this covenant is not a contract at all: it is a family bond. God makes a promise to Abraham to give him a family, and then promises to be part of that family - in fact, to be the true Father of the family. It is a promise that he fulfils definitively in the saving work of his only Son, whom he sends into the world out of love for us. By his Death and Resurrection, Jesus Christ, the Only Begotten Son of God, gives us new life and makes us sons and daughters of God by the grace of adoption.

The challenge of our lives as disciples - which we are renewing during Lent - is to see this extraordinary relationship to which God invites us, and to respond to it, to live as his children. It seems like a wonderful gift, of course, and yet we sometimes hesitate to accept it or to embrace it fully. As long as God is at some distance from us, we can have part of our lives for worship and prayer, and still keep part for ourselves. If we are truly family, however, then everything changes. It is not enough to show love and obedience on occasion, when it suits us. Rather, we have to obey the Lord *day by day*. We must love and respect him day by day. We must learn to love those whom he loves, who are brothers and sisters to us, day by day, in every ordinary choice and interaction.

Lest this seem burdensome, even overwhelming, our family relationship with the Lord gives us the right spirit in which to carry out our obligations to him. As the *Prayer over the People* suggests, we do not avoid sin merely to avoid breaking a commandment, but because it *does not please* the Father whom we love. We do what is right, not merely because of some external law, but because it *fills* us *with delight* to cooperate with him.

The Jewish leaders treated Jesus as a blasphemer when he acknowledged that the One God is truly his Father. Far from blasphemy, though, he was in fact revealing a glorious truth much deeper than anything they could have imagined. Not only is he truly the Son of God, but he desires to share that privilege with us. Not only is God his Father - by his Paschal Mystery the Lord Jesus makes God our Father as well.

Friday of the Fifth Week of Lent

Grant, we pray, almighty God,
that your servants, who seek the grace
    of your protection,
may be free from every evil
and serve you in peace of mind.
Through Christ our Lord.

Jr 20:10-13; Ps 18; Jn 10:31-42

∽

What keeps us from doing God's will? From drawing closer to him? From loving him sincerely? From loving our neighbours as we should? Temptation, of course, and the habits of sin that we have acquired, become obstacles to holiness. Spiritual wounds paralyse us as well: being hurt by someone makes us want to react badly, to trust less easily, to stay frozen in pain or anger. Fatigue, boredom, and discouragement when we don't see the results of our efforts to do good and to be good can prompt us to want to give up altogether. Sometimes the apparent fact that no one else seems to care if we are doing good, or everyone seems content not to do it, can be a convenient excuse to give up the fight. We can find ourselves feeling like Jeremiah, surrounded by a crowd of whispering enemies, afraid to make a move because we feel trapped or under attack.

102

The *Prayer over the People* today asks for a gift from God that is essential if we are to do his will: *peace of mind*. It is so difficult to hear the Lord's voice if our minds and hearts are not at peace, not able to listen amid the noise of the world and the whisperings of temptations and desires. The prayer asks that God set his *servants ... free from every evil*, and so make us able to *serve* him *in peace of mind*.

The source of our peace is the same that Jeremiah found and that Jesus proclaimed: knowledge of the Lord and of our relationship with him. "The Lord is at my side, a mighty hero," the prophet acknowledged, and so he knew that, whatever plots were being hatched against him, in the end they would come to nothing. "Believe in the work I do," Jesus insists, so that we can understand who he is, and that he comes to save us. More than that, in fact: he promises that if we believe in him, we will become "sons of God", sharing in the life that he will win for us by his greatest work, his Passion, Death and Resurrection.

Trials will still come; life will often be a battle. But if we keep our eye on the identity of God, on his works in our life, on our exalted vocation, we will not have to be filled with fear of our enemies, but rejoice in *the grace of* God's *protection* and serve him with peaceful hearts.

Saturday of the Fifth Week of Lent

Have mercy, Lord, on your Church,
as she brings you her supplications,
and be attentive to those who incline their hearts
    before you:
do not allow, we pray, those you have redeemed
by the Death of your Only Begotten Son,
to be harmed by their sins or weighed down
    by their trials.
Through Christ our Lord.

                    Ezk 37:21-38; Jr 31:10-13; Jn 11:45-56

In the Gospel today we hear all of the frustration and anger that has been building among the members of the Sanhedrin because of their controversies with Jesus finally come to a head. The reading focuses on the words of Caiaphas, the high priest, who says what nearly everyone had been thinking: we need to kill this Jesus, and to do it quickly.

John takes pains to tell us, however, why Caiaphas said what he did. It wasn't just his own sentiment, nor words simply to please the Sanhedrin or advance his own agenda. Rather, his words were a prophecy, John tells us, and so we need to look for a deeper meaning. John tells us that, too: Christ will indeed die, one for the sake of the many. By his death he will bring benefits that neither the high priest nor anyone there that day could ever have seen or imagined, beginning with unity, life and peace.

Thus, John shows us that the Passion was not something that just happened to Jesus, but rather the plan of God that he freely embraced. As Jesus says in another place in John's Gospel, "No one takes [my life] from me; I lay it down of my own free will, and as I have power to lay it down, so I have power to take it up again" (*Jn* 10:18). At the time he said it, the Pharisees said he was mad. We know instead that this attitude makes all the difference in how we bear the cross.

The *Prayer over the People* asks for God's help to do just that, and mentions our need for his grace so that we will not be *weighed down by trials*. But the way to avoid this kind of bending under the weight of the cross is to learn to bend another way: to *incline* our *hearts before* the Lord. Trials will come - the world is broken by sin and death. Either we freely submit to the Lord's plan and incline our hearts to him, or we grumble under the weight of our trials as if they are something imposed or inflicted upon us. This makes all the difference between carrying the cross all by ourselves, or sharing the burden with the Lord, who loved us enough to lay down his life for us all.

Palm Sunday of the Passion of the Lord

Look, we pray, O Lord, on this your family,
for whom our Lord Jesus Christ
did not hesitate to be delivered into the hands
  of the wicked
and submit to the agony of the Cross.
Who lives and reigns for ever and ever.

Mt 21:1-11 / Mk 11:1-10 or Jn 12:12-16 / Lk 19:28-40
Is 50:4-7; Ps 22; Ph 2:6-11
Mt 26:14-27:66 / Mk 14:1-15:47 / Lk 22:14-23:56

∽

The colt, the donkey's foal that figures so prominently in the first of the two Gospels for Palm Sunday, is almost as famous as its rider. Like him, it figures in Old Testament prophecies: Matthew and John both point explicitly to Zechariah 9:9 - "Rejoice heart and soul, daughter of Zion! Shout for joy, daughter of Jerusalem! Look, your king is approaching, he is vindicated and victorious, humble and riding on a donkey, on a colt, the foal of a donkey." Those who shouted "Hosanna to the Son of David" may have been thinking of the passage in the First Book of Kings (1:32-34) that tells how David gave instructions that his son Solomon should be seated on David's own mule, and

process to the place where he would be anointed king. Centuries before either of these passages, moreover, was the blessing of Jacob for his son, Judah. "The sceptre shall not pass from Judah, nor the ruler's staff from between his feet … He tethers his donkey to the vine, to its stock the foal of his she-donkey" (*Gn* 49:10-11).

So, the Palm Sunday donkey was certainly significant - foretold in prophecies, commandeered by the Master, it was already in a special category. Then it entered Jerusalem amid shouts of triumph. It walked on soft cloaks, amid waving branches and an adoring throng. It must have been quite an experience for its first time carrying someone on its back.

But suppose, in the midst of this excitement, the donkey were to raise its head, to look around and begin to nod in acknowledgement of the adulation of the crowd. What a fool it would be, and how foolish it would appear to them! Their praises were not for the donkey, but for the One whom it was bearing. The job of the animal was simply to carry Jesus on his way, not to draw attention to itself.

Our calling as Christians is to bear Jesus in our hearts, and thus to bring him to others. In these days of Holy Week we need to be ever more aware of this vocation of ours, and strive to live by it. No matter how jaded the world becomes, it still watches the Church during Holy Week. Despite its penchant for telling bad news, there will still be coverage in the media of these most solemn liturgies.

There is no question that the eyes of the world are upon us; but for what purpose?

Many people may be looking for another reason to reject Christ and his Church. We must not give them one. Others are questioning, seeking a way to find out who God is and how to respond to him. If we bear Christ faithfully, we can lead others to know him better. But always this means showing people Jesus, leading them to him and not to ourselves. This requires bearing also the daily crosses of detachment and humility.

We can find strength to bear these burdens because the eyes of someone else are on us. The *Prayer over the People* doesn't make specific petitions today, except that the Lord would *look on this,* his *family*, recalling what Christ his Son did for us. In that look of love we find that we are known and loved by him, and we find courage and grace to love him and to seek his will.

A medieval legend draws our eyes to the dark stripes of hair that appear on a donkey's back: one down the spine, another across the shoulders. It encourages us to see this cross as a gift from the Lord, to recall the day that its ancestor willingly bore the Son of David to the place where he would take up his cross for us. We also are marked by the cross of Christ, singled out with the responsibility of bearing him to others. The knowledge that he is with us, and that he has called us, empowers us to lay down our lives in humility, and to lead others to him.

Monday of Holy Week

May your protection, O Lord, we pray,
defend the humble
and keep ever safe those who trust in your mercy,
that they may celebrate the paschal festivities
not only with bodily observance
but above all with purity of mind.
Through Christ our Lord.

Is 42:1-7; *Ps* 27; *Jn* 12:1-11

∞

Our readings for the next few days will focus on the figure of Judas - what he was like, what his personality was - as if the Gospels and the Church are trying to give us some context in which to understand his actions. Perhaps it is more difficult, though, to comprehend the actions of Jesus. Surely he knew what Judas was like. Why did he not distance himself from him, ask him to depart?

One reason we could suggest, of course, is that the betrayal of Jesus was all part of the plan, and there is a mysterious way in which surely this is true. We also have to remember that Jesus is the Lord who *defends the humble*, who does not quench the smouldering wick or break the bruised reed. Right to the very moment that he betrayed Jesus, Judas always had the freedom to reject the temptation and to do what was right. Even afterwards, he had the chance, like Peter and the rest of the Twelve, to turn back and receive forgiveness from the Risen Lord.

But we know what happened, and to a large extent we know why: Judas, who had seen Christ's miracles, would not let his own blindness be healed. He would not *trust in* the Lord's *mercy*, would not follow Jesus out of his confining attitudes. This is why the *Prayer over the People* asks God today not only for the strength to do good, *but above all* for *purity of mind*. If we would serve Christ, like Mary of Bethany did, we must hold nothing back, but let him change our minds and our perspective. Then we can approach the Lord - in the Sacraments, in his Word, in the poor. Then we can perceive the meaning of his Passion, Death and Resurrection, and celebrate with festive joy the redemption he won for us by the events of that first Holy Week.

Tuesday of Holy Week

May your mercy, O God,
cleanse the people that are subject to you
from all seduction of former ways
and make them capable of new holiness.
Through Christ our Lord.

Is 49:1-6; *Ps* 71; *Jn* 13:21-33,36-38

∽

In the First Reading today we hear the second of what have come to be known as the Songs of the Suffering Servant. They point the way to Jesus, who is sent by his Father to redeem the People of God by taking their burden of sin on himself. This prophecy shows us the identity of the Lord as one who proclaims a message of repentance, and specifically of *return*. He takes on his mission so "that Jacob may be brought back to him, and Israel returned to him". He carries out this mission even when he doesn't see immediate results, knowing that when it seems he is working uselessly, even then he is doing the Father's will.

At the end of the reading, the Servant of the Lord receives a new aspect to his mission. "It is not enough" for him to call back the Israelites who have strayed from the Lord. He will also extend an invitation to "the nations, ...

to the ends of the earth", that all may hear the Word of the Lord and obtain salvation. The merciful love of God is abundant, overflowing. It is not only healing but also creative. It always reaches out further, to draw all people to himself.

We have been hard at work this Lent trying to be converted - to overcome the *seduction of former ways* that keep us attached to sin and to worldly things. The Lord blesses our efforts and gives healing and *cleansing*, but, as the mission of the Suffering Servant reveals to us, ultimately he wants more than that. It is not enough simply to return to him; he wants us then to move forward with him along the path he has chosen for us. It is not enough to turn from former ways; he wants to *make* us *capable of new holiness*.

We see the glory of Jesus when he lays down his life, as the Servant of the Lord, to save us from our sins. He gives us a share in the redemption he has won, and this truly does save us from sin. But he also wants to give us a share in his glory, and for that we must not only come back to him, but stay with him, and walk with him the way of holiness.

Wednesday of Holy Week

Grant your faithful, O Lord, we pray,
to partake unceasingly of the paschal mysteries
and to await with longing the gifts to come,
that, persevering in the Sacraments of their rebirth,
they may be led by Lenten works to newness of life.
Through Christ our Lord.

Is 50:4-9a; Ps 69; Mt 26:14-25

∞

It was bound to happen, with twelve men in charge of things. It is not as if they didn't know it was coming, or that it would have been too complicated to arrange. They were busy, of course, but this was something terribly important. Yet, Matthew tells us, it wasn't until "the first day of the Feast of Unleavened Bread" that the disciples came to Jesus to talk about getting the Passover supper ready! Thankfully, as usual, Christ has everything prepared, and can simply send them to a certain house, a certain host; and they find that Jesus has thought of everything. The apostles may have been late, but the Lord Jesus is always at work, providing everything necessary, so that they can celebrate what will be their Last Supper with him, and so that he can transform their lives.

Hopefully we have been faithful to the *Lenten works* of penance and preparation that we undertook six weeks ago. Hopefully we find ourselves ready for the Sacred Triduum that begins tomorrow evening. Suppose, though, that we are not as ready as we might be, that the busyness of daily life, or something more serious, has overcome our best intentions? The example of the apostles can reassure us (as usual) and encourage us to recognise the ways that the Lord has been at work in us. Perhaps we have been less than mindful in recent weeks. Still, the invitation remains to focus on his love for us, and take at least the next few days to celebrate his gift.

As it did for the apostles, Christ's gift of himself has the power to transform our lives. The *Prayer over the People* asks God for the help we need to keep *persevering in the Sacraments of rebirth* that make us disciples, that enable us to hope in God and long for his kingdom. In this way, we take part in the mysteries of his self-sacrificing gift, not only in these holy days, but *unceasingly*, in every place, at every moment.

Ready or not, we must enter into these next few days, with faith and hope, not discouragement. We must recognise that, as usual, it is what Christ is doing, rather than what we have done, that really makes the difference. And what a difference, what a transformation it will make in our lives, if we truly spend these days with him.

Holy Thursday of the Lord's Supper

*O God, who have called us to participate
in this most sacred Supper,
in which your Only Begotten Son,
when about to hand himself over to death,
entrusted to the Church a sacrifice new for all eternity,
the banquet of his love,
grant we pray,
that we may draw from so great a mystery,
the fullness of charity and life.
Through Christ our Lord.*

(Collect of the Mass of the Lord's Supper)

Ex 12:1-8,11-14; *Ps* 116; *1 Co* 11:23-26; *Jn* 13:1-15

The Opening Prayer (or Collect) for this evening's Mass reiterates what we celebrate whenever we come to the altar: the *sacrifice new for all eternity* which the Lord gave us when he sacrificed himself to feed us at *the banquet of his love*. And so the First Reading relates God's own instructions for the sacrifice at the heart of the great covenant he made with his people as he brought them out of slavery. As we celebrate the new and eternal covenant, we recognise Jesus Christ as the fulfilment of everything foreshadowed in the Old Testament, and above all as the true Paschal Lamb.

Our celebration and adoration of the Lamb of God actually began a few days ago. Last Sunday we acknowledged Jesus as the Son of David and the one who was to come into the world, as we recalled his triumphant entrance into his own royal city, Jerusalem. Mark tells us that this took place late in the day (*Mk* 11:11) - that is, at the beginning of the tenth day of the first lunar month. Saint Bede and other Fathers of the Church want us to pay attention and see that this tenth day was the one on which the Israelites were commanded to "procure for [themselves] a lamb". They kept it until it was sacrificed four days later in the evening twilight. Tonight we offer the true Paschal Lamb, the Lamb of God, but only because he freely gave himself to us to be our sacrifice of redemption.

God commanded Moses to offer "lambs without blemish", and we know that it is the sinless obedience of Our Lord, our Lamb, that saves us from the death of sin. But how can we offer his sacrifice if we are not as pure as he? The Book of Exodus tells us that the Israelites were allowed to choose the lamb from the sheep or the goats, and Saint Augustine sees a great mystery here. Sometimes we come before the Lord full of charity, purity and innocence, like the quiet, docile sheep. At other times our sins make us like the goats; but if we come before the Lord with repentance and ask for his mercy and forgiveness, he welcomes us also to his altar. He not only cleanses us from our sins, but makes us like himself.

This is the greatest mystery of the Most Blessed Sacrament, that it is as members of the flock that we offer up the Lamb of God. He has become like us, to the point of taking on our weakness and our mortality, so that we can become like him, members of his body and adopted sons and daughters of his Father. So our sharing in this meal unites us not only with him, but, in *the fullness of charity and of life*, it binds us together with one another. We partake of the Lamb as one family, one household. We eat it together with the bread of necessity amid the bitterness of life, and the Lamb himself teaches us to reach out to those afflicted by poverty and pain.

We are called to eat the Paschal meal girded for travel, because we have a journey to make. The full light of Christ shows us where we are heading, out into a world full of evil and sorrow, but redeemed by the sacrifice of Christ. We are sent to bring the message of his Gospel, the news of his Passion, to bring his own hope and love, following the Lamb wherever he goes.

Good Friday of the Passion of the Lord

May abundant blessing, O Lord, we pray,
descend upon your people,
who have honoured the Death of your Son
in the hope of their resurrection:
may pardon come,
comfort be given,
holy faith increase,
and everlasting redemption be made secure.
Through Christ our Lord.

   Is 52:13-53:12; *Ps* 31; *Heb* 4:14-16;5:7-9; *Jn* 18:1-19:42

What a gift it is from the Lord God to have not one, but four Gospels, each written by an inspired human author with his own perspective and technique. Even with an event as important and central to the faith as the Passion of the Lord, the four evangelists each provide unique details. In doing so, they draw our attention to specific aspects of the story they consider important, and this is especially true when all four of them include the same person or event. One example from the accounts of the Passion is the cock that crowed at the moment of Peter's denial of the Lord Jesus. Not only is it consistently reported in all four

Gospels, but Jesus himself specifically predicted it during the Last Supper.

When we contemplate the Passion, *honouring the death of* the *Son* of God, we are confronted by so much darkness: the darkness of evil and sin, of cowardice and indifference, of jealousy and hatred, of suffering, pain, abandonment and grief. It can cast our own minds and hearts into shadow, and leave us confused and doubting. So it is not difficult to sympathise with Peter, accosted in the dark and the cold, overwhelmed with grief and fear, as he reacts to the accusations of the crowd, and denies Jesus to save his own skin.

And then the cock crows. The many species of birds in the world tend to have one thing in common: when it is dark, they do not move, and they don't make a sound. The cock cries out, however, and becomes the first to herald and proclaim the truth that makes this a truly Good Friday. From its vantage point, it sees first what no one else can perceive, and it knows one thing for certain: the light has come; a new day is dawning.

Only eyes of holy faith can see it, but the truth is there. What Jesus did on the cross, for us, begins a new day - the old night of sin has ended. We are still waiting to see the daylight in its fullness, when the Light of the World comes forth from the tomb. But even now we can recognise the first glimmer of the new light. His death brings us pardon; his suffering gives us comfort; his self-sacrifice secures our redemption, and makes us one with him.

The Death and Resurrection of Christ changes everything, for us and for the world. We must live like we too can see the light, and must announce it to others.

One small animal giving testimony that a new day was dawning caused a complete transformation in Peter, one that saved his relationship with Jesus, and likely saved his life. Imagine what a transformation in the world we could bring about if we live like we are forgiven, and extend God's mercy even to our enemies. Imagine how bright the world will become when we give witness by our words and actions that, although things still seem quite dark, even now the day is breaking, and the Light of Christ is coming to those who will receive him.

Even in the darkness of our own sins, amid the shadows in which we hide to do our own will and to save our own skins, Christ calls to us from the cross and invites us to live in his light. This day, this very good day, is the first day of eternal life. Let us welcome it with gladness, and proclaim it to all we meet.

Easter Sunday of the Resurrection of the Lord

The Easter Vigil in the Holy Night

Gn 1:1-2:2; *Gn* 22:1-18; *Ex* 14:15-15:1; *Is* 54:5-14
Is 55:1-11; *Ba* 3:9-15,32-4:4; *Ezk* 36:16-17a,18-28
Rm 6:3-11; *Ps* 118
Mt 28:1-10 / *Mk* 16:1-7 / *Lk* 24:1-12

Easter Sunday

Ac 10:34a,37-43; *Ps* 118; *Col* 3:1-4 or *1 Co* 5:6b-8; *Jn* 20:1-9

∞

The Easter Vigil is a unique celebration in the Church's liturgical year. Many more passages from Scripture than usual are read at this Mass. The Sacraments of Initiation are celebrated during the Mass. The congregation is sprinkled with holy water as a symbol of the Baptismal promises they have just renewed. But perhaps the most dramatic part comes at the very beginning of the liturgy, as the flame from a new fire is first used to light the Paschal candle, and then is passed from person to person until the whole assembly is bearing the light. There is a great mystery in this symbol, which speaks about our lives as disciples of the Risen One.

The *Exultet*, the Easter Proclamation, highlights this mystery among the many praises it makes of the Paschal candle that represents Christ our Light. "Now we know the praises of this pillar," it says, "which glowing fire ignites for God's honour; a fire into many flames divided, yet never dimmed by sharing of its light." When we received the gift of eternal life at Baptism, by dying and rising with Christ Jesus, we received the gift of sanctifying grace, a share in God's own life. He makes this gift to us without diminishing himself. Just like this, we are called to share God's life with others - to share his love, his mercy and his forgiveness, his compassion and joy, his encouragement and strength.

At times we might hesitate to respond to this call, mindful of the sacrifices and the work involved. We may worry that we will not have the strength or the energy to undertake the task. But the many flames remind us that we are not diminished by sharing love. Rather, it is in making a gift of ourselves that we become who we were created to be. Our sacrifices and labour in Christ's service are a source of strength and joy for us as well as for those whom we serve.

The *Exultet* goes on to explain the source of the candle's strength, in words that we did not hear in English until the new translation of the third edition of the *Roman Missal*. The candle, it says, "is fed by melting wax, drawn out by mother bees to build a torch so precious". We have learnt this week from the Palm Sunday donkey, from the Paschal lamb, from the cock that crowed early on Good Friday. Can the Easter bees teach us anything about how to serve and follow Christ?

The bees "draw out" the wax to make the candle, we hear. Draw it out from where, exactly? From lots of places, it turns out: from this flower and that, they are always at work collecting as much nectar as they can, and taking it back to their home. In sacred art, this trait has long made bees a symbol of industriousness and wisdom: they look for all the best, wherever it is to be found, and work hard to obtain it.

The Liturgy of the Word at the Easter Vigil presents us with many varied stories and prophecies, many words of prayer and praise from the Psalms. Yet we know it is only a tiny fraction of what is contained in God's Word for us. When we are diligently attentive to the many places that the Word of God is to be found - in the Scripture, the teaching of the Church, the experiences of prayer in daily life - then we recognise Christ in our midst. We learn his love and his wisdom, and we draw strength to carry out his will.

The purpose of all this drawing out and gathering in, the *Exultet* says, was to build "this precious torch". But what bee in a hive could ever think of such a thing? It can be tiring, frustrating, even boring to do our daily duties toward God and neighbour, particularly when we don't perceive results from our efforts. Only eyes of faith and hope can look ahead to see that God is making something beautiful out of our efforts to serve him - even when we are only a small part of his great plan.

The *Exultet* does not sing about a rather sombre truth, which nevertheless is very real: the Paschal candle is not hive-shaped. The only way that the "work of bees" becomes this precious sign is when those bees allow their work, their very home, to be destroyed, then purified, and then reshaped according to a plan and purpose. Discipleship likewise requires that we hand over to the Lord all the plans that we have made for ourselves, all the worldly things and comforts with which we have surrounded ourselves - that we die to self and let Christ purify our hearts. Yet after every daily dying to self comes a resurrection, as Christ shapes and moulds us into disciples who can bear his light to the world.

Easter is *for us*. Resurrection is *for us*. The Passion and Death of Christ are *for us*. By them he makes us his own, and sends us out for the sake of others. He enlightens our souls with his risen glory, so that we can find our joy, our light, our life in him, and by imitating his love we can spread his light.

Conclusion

Go forth and announce the Gospel of the Lord.

⚭

Each day of this Lent, we have received the special blessing of the Church at the end of Mass, to strengthen and support us on our journey of penance and conversion. Through the *Prayers over the People*, the Church has asked God to purify our hearts, to enlighten our minds, and to make us more aware of his action in our lives. These prayers were certainly addressed to God, the source of every gift and blessing, but they also contained messages for us, shaping our public and private prayer and opening our hearts to receive God's gifts. They sent us back to our homes and workplaces with spiritual food and encouragement.

Now that we have reached the goal of our Lenten striving, we rejoice in the glory of Easter with renewed commitment to the promises of faith we first made at Baptism. Our journey of discipleship is not over, however. On the contrary: our celebration of the Resurrection of the Lord has just begun, and will continue during the fifty days that culminate in the solemn feast of Pentecost. More importantly, our vocation to bear witness to the reality